To my family.

D360

Nine Conversations about Whole-life Discipleship

Gregory Koenig

D360: Nine Conversations About Whole-life Discipleship
Copyright © 2016 Gregory Koenig
April 2016
ISBN-13: 978-1530836772
ISBN-10: 1530836778

Table of Contents

3

Introduction

I serve an organization whose mission is "equipping leaders to make disciples who make disciples on campus." Not long ago, during a conference presentation on leader development, I was making some generic remarks about disciple-building, and one participant stopped me to ask what I considered the characteristics of a "disciple." I was ready with a few—studying God's Word, being active in Christian community, growing closer to God through prayer, presenting a living, active witness.... I explained that this was a big topic and my list was only a partial one. After considering for a moment, the participant replied, "I think it would be really helpful—to me at least—to be able to see the full picture as your organization understands it."

That got me to thinking: as good as we Jesus-followers are at *talking about making disciples* (we can all recite the "make disciples" verse from Matthew, right?), how good are we at knowing what a disciple is and how to help people become disciples?

My questions turned into a research project—and after digging deeper than I ever had before, I had three reactions to what I found.

Reaction 1: Building disciples ... or church members?

The first reaction is one that I believe is shared by more than one other follower of Jesus—perhaps by a lot more:

Jesus commanded His disciples in Matthew 28 to help others develop as disciples. Many churches today, including churches I've been part of, are quite adept at producing church members but not at discipling. Of course, some people claim that when you're a church member, you're also a disciple. I humbly disagree, and apparently discipleship thought leader Mike Breen does, too. He says, "If you make disciples, you always get the church. But if you make a church, you rarely get disciples."[1] In fact, I'm convinced you can run people through Sunday school, Christian school, confirmation classes, adult instruction classes, new member classes, and you-name-it classes, and at the end certify that all the participants have met the requirements for membership—and still not necessarily have any more disciples than you started with. So I became convinced that there truly is a difference between a church member and a disciple of Jesus—and began to concentrate on how developing a disciple might be a different process from producing a church member. This reaction has a second dimension. I have noticed that a growing number of congregations and traditional Christian organizations have recently revitalized and intensified their evangelistic outreach in North America. That's great, and it could indeed bring in a lot of people who otherwise might not have found their way to church. But it's here that Mike Breen's remark resonates with me in a second way. If Breen is right, churches need to be locked and loaded to begin *discipling* these people the moment they set foot in the door—or many will become church members with little hope of growing into disciples; or perhaps they will be members for a short time and then fade away. If you evangelize just to make the church, you will seldom get disciples. Churches that evangelize need to be ready to engage new people in discipleship ministry right away—rather than pour all their effort into making them eligible for membership and then leaving it to them to figure out how to be disciples (or even to sense that being a disciple is something bigger and deeper). This is something that churches do all too often.

Reaction 2: Discipleship is more than running a "spiritual disciplines" checklist, isn't it?

As the sense of the "member vs. disciple" disconnect started to grow in me, one of the first resources I discovered was a kind of handbook that directs the prospective disciple to incorporate an impressive list of "disciplines" into his or her life. I recognize that the words "disciple" and "discipline" are inextricably related and that much of discipleship does indeed involve embracing certain disciplines. But the list of disciplines in the book was long and, to my mind, over-scrupulous and even tedious. I didn't finish the book; it just didn't present the picture of discipleship that was becoming clear to me from another book I was reading—the Bible.

Reaction 3: New models—innovative methods for discipling at the church level, but …

During my research I discovered that some very creative new models for discipling within the context of the church have emerged; in general, they are exciting to read about. But just as I was certain I was not looking for a complex and exacting checklist of spiritual disciplines to impose over my growing desire for discipleship, so I was also not necessarily looking for innovative new methods for building a culture of discipleship at the church level. Building a culture of discipleship is good, and it's what I would want to see in a church I belong to. But in that moment, rebuilding my church's culture was not my top priority; this was a personal quest. So I set those great discipling-culture resources aside.

What I was in search of, I believe, was ways of expressing how to wrap everything I think and do in the commitment to follow Jesus. How deep, how rich, how revitalizing, how restorative, how mobilizing could that be? So that's my intention for this book: to present, with a minimum of churchy language, nine conversations about what living our whole lives as disciples of Jesus could look like—could mean. My hope and prayer are that these conversations will help you sort out your own understanding of what being a disciple is all about, stir your desire to live your life as a disciple of Jesus, stimulate in you a hunger to learn more, and guide you as you respond to God's call to help others grow as disciples.

Assumptions

There are some things that many—I think most—human beings wrestle with at some point. One is whether there is some force or entity that is greater than each of us and all of us. Another is our purpose for being. A third is why things are the way they are. And a fourth is comprised of things associated with the end of life that we can't control:

- whether or not each of us has a soul that lives on after physical death;
- whether or not heaven and hell exist;

- who will judge each of us when life ends;
- what that judgment will be.

I believe that God has a plan for humanity concerning these things and that His advice to humanity about them can be found in the Bible.

My belief is founded on several assumptions:

- God exists. This pretty much answers the first concern I mentioned.
- What we read in the Bible is true.
- If what we read in the Bible is true, then what the Bible says about itself—that it is a single, unified message inspired by the Holy Spirit to teach humans how God has restored humanity's relationship with Him—is also true. In light of this, the Bible is assumed to be an authoritative historical record.
- And if what we read in the Bible is true, then Jesus' characterization of God as one God but three persons—Father, Son and Holy Spirit—is accurate.
- Further, if what we read in the Bible is true, then God created everything.
- God is the ultimate objective truth. This resolves the apparent circularity of the truth of the Bible and the existence of God (That is, it's a circular argument that the Bible is true because God is its

source, and God is Who we believe He is because the Bible says so.)

- Jesus was a real human person. He was also a unique person—fully human but also fully God.

All the assumptions I've listed are made on faith, which I trust to be a real thing. Incidentally, faith is not something that only Christians, or only religious people, have. Many people who believe in empirical science—or who believe in nothing at all—still accept and assume things on faith. Unverified (and unverifiable) scientific theories that evolve over time into "empirical truth" are actually rooted not in observable fact but in people's faith in things such as the scientific method and uniformitarianism. Some readers will not simply accept these assumptions. That's all right; skepticism is a natural reaction to claims such as these. But ultimately, a person's lack of acceptance does not negate the truth I apprehend in the Bible. I invite you to study the Bible carefully and check out these assumptions for yourself.

Note

One

In the Image

Imagine there was an all-powerful Being, let's accord Him the title of God, Who created everything out of nothing. Imagine that God took the earth when it was empty and shapeless, and made it into the perfect place to sustain life—and then created life. Imagine that God then made human beings as His crowning achievement—a special creature made in His image, that is, imbued with traits of His own unique character, such as knowledge and wisdom and creativity and cleverness and caring and compassion and humor and generosity and more—and, above all, love. Imagine too that He added the special, exclusive ability for humans to choose whether to live in harmonious relationship with Him or to live in rebellion, apart from Him.

Imagine that as the almighty king of this good kingdom ("very good," Genesis 1:31), God chose humans—a man, whom He created first, and a woman, created to complete the man and to be his helper for life—to rule alongside Him. Imagine that He placed them in an idyllic garden, where they could live in harmony with the rest of His creation—and where they could even exercise the choice He gave them to live with Him or to live without Him.

Of course, if you have grown up with the book we call the Bible[1] as part of your life, you don't have to imagine any of this—because it's a summary of the creation story as it is found in Genesis 1 and 2. And as you may be thinking, there's even more to the story. We'll return to that shortly.

Wrong Story?

Now, you'll recall this series of conversations is about developing as a disciple of Jesus—so it would be fair if you were to ask what the primeval creation story from Genesis has to do with that. After all, you have to read 38 more books—the rest of the whole Old Testament—before Jesus even shows up, right?

Apart from the fact that the Son and the Holy Spirit were together with the Father at creation, and apart from the episodes in the Old Testament where a character called "the angel of the LORD" is claimed to be the "preincarnate Christ" (we will not be talking about the preincarnate Christ in any of our conversations), yes, it's true that Jesus does not show up in person before the first book of the New Testament, the gospel of Matthew. So what's up with the Genesis history? Stick with me.

Let's look for a moment at the idea of being a disciple of Jesus. In the first century, disciples followed rabbis, and Jesus was considered a rabbi. A rabbi would invite a gifted young man to "follow" him—with the intention of training the gifted young man to be like him and to do the same things he could do. When Jesus called young men in Galilee to be his disciples (although they may not have been "gifted" in the way the term was understood), that's one of the things each of them expected—that Jesus would teach them to be like Him and to do the things He could do.

And when Jesus stood on a mountain in Galilee and gave His apostles the command to "disciple all nations" (Matthew 28:18-20), the expectation was the same—that they would train people everywhere to be like Jesus and to do the things He could do.

But while they were with Jesus up on that mountain, in spite of all they had witnessed, His disciples were still not clear about what being and making disciples of Jesus would actually entail. "Is this the time when you're going to restore the kingdom to Israel?" they asked (Acts 1:6). They were convinced He was the long-promised Messiah. In the mind of a first-century Jew, the Messiah would come to end foreign domination of Israel and re-establish the rightful rule of the house of David. And in their minds, they, the disciples of the Messiah, were to learn how to do this and to carry on His work.

Jesus was all about restoring a kingdom, of course; he was always talking about it: "first, be concerned about his [the Father's] kingdom" (Matthew 6:33); "Jesus went to all the towns and villages. He taught in the synagogues and spread the Good News of the kingdom" (Matthew 9:35); "No one can enter the kingdom of God without being born of water and the Spirit" (John 3:5). But the kingdom He had in mind wasn't the one the disciples assumed He was referring to: as He had told Pontius Pilate, "My kingdom does not belong to this world" (John 18:36).

Back to the creation story.

There IS Only One Story: Restoring the Kingdom —Beginning with Humans

The book of Genesis reports that the first humans did indeed exercise the power of choice that God had given them—and that they chose poorly.[2] Their rejection of God's covenant with them was what has come to be called sin.

Everything changed:

> Sin came into the world through one person, and death came through sin. So death spread to everyone, because everyone sinned. (Romans 5:12)

You'll recall that earlier I described humans as God's crowning achievement, created in His own image, "imbued with traits of His own unique character—knowledge and wisdom and creativity ... and, above all, love." When humans chose to reject living in harmony with God in His perfect kingdom, the image of Himself with which God had endowed them was damaged, and it would be flawed in almost every human born afterward (in fact, with only one exception).

Yet while it was flawed, the image of God in humans wasn't destroyed completely, nor did it fade away and die in the generations that followed.

Think about it.

If someone were to ask you if you believe our life on earth is as good as it could possibly be, what would your answer be? Wouldn't you say *no*? What do you think most people would say? Many—maybe most—people will agree that things are not as good as they could be—that there's a lot in this world that is actually broken.

How is it that so many people would think that? What makes so many of us think, "There's something better, I know it—if I could just get to it"?

Think about some other questions:

- How do I know what good is? What evil is?
- How do I know love when I experience it?

- What motivates me to ...
  ... desire authentic relationship?
  ... seek community with other people?
  ... desire to create? To succeed? To excel? To
  transcend?
  ... desire to make the world a better place?
  ... pray?
  ... expect, and act with, justice and fairness?
  ... believe in things that don't appear to make
  rational sense?

What is the source of these knowledges and motivations? Instinct? Our species' advanced state of evolution? Its more ambitious climb up Abraham Maslow's hierarchy of needs?

Really?

Or could the source be what remains of the image of God in us?

The image of Himself that God placed in the first humans is (still) in all humans, no matter where they are, no matter where they were born and grew up, no matter what they believe in — if they believe in anything. In fact, the apostle Paul hints at this reality when he talks about how people who were not given God's law manage somehow to obey it:

> [W]henever non-Jews who don't have the laws in
> Moses' Teachings do by nature the things that

those laws contain, they are a law to themselves
even though they don't have any of those laws.
They show that some requirements found in
Moses' Teachings are written in their hearts. Their
consciences speak to them. (Romans 2:14-15)

That is, some of God's expectations remain "written
on the heart" of every human being. They can be understood to be a vestige of His image. We simply call
them our conscience.[3]

True, the image of God in humans has been stifled
and enfeebled and flawed by the sinful nature we
inherited from the very first humans—and by our
own disobedience—which is why we also have war
and crime and brutality and racism and neglect and
starvation and exploitation and injustice and greed
(and even more stuff that separates us from God, of
course). But we read that when God created humans,
He made His image an integral part of this unique
creation. And He didn't *uncreate* humans when they
rebelled. Once long ago He destroyed all but eight
humans, yes. But He never uncreated humanity.
Which, it can be argued, suggests that He never re-
moved the image of Himself in which He had created the first humans.

Instead, He has been, and still is, on a crusade
(quite literally a crusade; yep, that's a play on words)
to restore the kingdom He established so long ago—

beginning with humans and the image of Himself in all of us.

Before you go on, read that last sentence again and let it sink in.

Are we there yet?

So that's the mission Jesus was on. When He would go into towns and villages and tell the people, "Turn to God and change the way you think and act, because the kingdom of heaven is near!" (Matthew 4:17), it was this kingdom He was referring to. And, after all the generations that had passed, when the kingdom finally "came near" in the person of Jesus, God's project to restore His creation entered its next phase: redemption and regeneration of humans' souls.

In the first phase God had revealed His plan to restore His image in humans and restore all of His creation; He had chosen a family through which this phase of His plan would be carried out; and He had spent generations upon generations working to build a relationship with that family. This next phase—the redemption and regeneration of humans' souls— would be comparatively brief: God sent His Son to take on humanity as the man Jesus, to live a perfect life and to die a sacrificial death to atone for humans' rebellion—all of which occurred in the space of about thirty years. But it achieved for humanity something we humans could not do for ourselves; it took away the guilt of our sins so that God could once again consider humans "righteous," that is, "sin-less":

> Because all people have sinned, they have fallen short of God's glory. They receive God's approval freely by an act of his kindness through the price Christ Jesus paid to set us free from sin. (Romans 3:23-24).

And now God also considers those who believe this to be *worthy*—worthy to join Him in His restoration project! Think about the very first Christian believers—Jesus' own disciples. Jesus had trained them, even sending them out on field exercises; and when He had completed the task of redeeming and regenerating humanity through His death and resurrection, He wasted no time in declaring the disciples worthy to disciple more people—all people everywhere. They would be the ones to deliver His invitation to the world to accept the free gift of a restored relationship with God; they would be the ones to recruit everyone else into a whole-life partnership in restoring His image in humans and in working together to restore His creation, His kingdom.

So. Now. *The point: the project continues!* As the apostle Paul explains, all believers are called to have a role in it:

> Whoever is a believer in Christ is a new creation.... A new way of living has come into existence. God has done all this. He has restored our relationship with him through Christ, and has given us this ministry of restoring relationships. In other words, God was using Christ to restore his relationship with humanity. He didn't hold people's faults against them, and he has given us this message of restored relationships to tell others. Therefore, we are Christ's representatives, and through us God is calling you. (2 Corinthians 5:17-20a)

So what does this look like for you—this project of God's to restore His image in you and to partner with you in restoring creation? I can't paint a whole picture. God, in His infinite creativity, has made you unique; so for you, whoever you are, that picture will look different from everybody else's picture.

However, I can offer you some ideas and resources as you begin to envision your role in the project. Are you ready? Then let's proceed by going in depth with our central concept, *discipleship*.

Summary

God created everything. When He created human beings, He made them "in His image" (Genesis 1:26-27). The first humans made an unfortunate choice in rejecting God's agreement for living in the garden He created; ever since, the image of God in humans, together with all of God's creation, has been corrupt. God is on a mission to restore His creation, including the image of Himself in humans. He began by sending His Son, Jesus, to live a perfect life, die a sacrificial death, and rise from the dead to redeem humans and restore His relationship with them. Now He invites people who believe this to become disciples of Jesus and join Him in His restoration project.

But now you must also put away all the following: anger, wrath, malice, slander, and filthy language from your mouth. Do not lie to one another, since you have put off the old man with his practices and have put on the new man, who is being renewed in knowledge according to the image of his Creator. (2 Corinthians 3:8-10)

Deal With It

1. What does it mean to you that human beings have been "created in the image of God"? How do you know the image of God in humans has been corrupted ever since the earliest humans disobeyed God?

2. In his book *The Next Christians: Seven Ways You Can Live the Gospel and Restore the World*, Gabe Lyons

writes, "The next Christians believe that Christ's death and resurrection were not only meant to save people *from* something. He wanted to save Christians *to* something." Do you feel you have been "saved *to* something"? What's that mean for you?

Go and Do

At the end of each conversation in this series, you will be challenged to put some aspect of what you're learning into action—that is, to "Go and Do." Want to give it a try?

1. Look for an opportunity to ask someone you know what being "created in the image of God" means to him or her; as a follow-up, ask whether he or she believes people are still created in God's image. Don't feel as if you need to teach or preach; just listen. But if your friend asks to share what you think, feel free.

2. How would you complete this sentence: "As a human being whom Jesus has restored to His kingdom and blessed with unique gifts, I can join Jesus in His project to restore His creation by _____."

Two

Discipleship: A Life of Response to the Work of the Holy Spirit

As we begin, it's important to deal with what discipleship is not. Disciplines such as worship, Bible study and prayer—that is, things that you *do*—play a major role in your growth as a disciple of Jesus. Yet discipleship is not works-righteousness—attempting to persuade God to award you eternal life because of the good things you do. It doesn't work that way; as we saw in the preceding conversation, our flawed nature renders us incapable of obeying God to the degree He demands (perfection). For that matter, our flawed nature also renders us incapable of even deciding on our own to live our lives as disciples of Jesus.

But, first, as a believer, you know that you already have eternal life from God, given through the sacrificial death and victorious resurrection of Jesus—and you have received this free gift (in churchy language: *grace*) through faith. And second, when it comes to living your life as a disciple of Jesus, think about this little passage:

> I believe that I cannot by my own reason or strength believe in Jesus Christ, my Lord, or come to Him; but the Holy Spirit has called me by the Gospel, enlightened me with His gifts, sanctified and kept me in the true faith….

Perhaps you are familiar with these words. The Reformer Martin Luther wrote them to help explain the Third Article of the Apostles' Creed ("I believe in the Holy Spirit, the holy Christian church…").[1] Luther's explanation points to the one thing we need to understand as we get serious about living as disciples of Jesus Christ: it's God's Holy Spirit Who prepares our hearts and minds and Who calls us to faith and a life of discipleship in Jesus. And it is because of the Spirit's transforming work in us that each of us can respond with a life of authentic discipleship.

Read that last sentence again, because it's important.

So, then: what is a life of response to the Holy Spirit's work—what is a *disciple*?

Most people understand "disciple" to mean "follower," but what does that really mean?

Kyle Idleman is a pastor and the author of a study series titled *not a fan*.[2] In it he claims that many people are "fans" of Jesus—enthusiastic admirers:

people who believe what the Bible says about Jesus, who think church is a great idea and go whenever they can, who buy—and wear—the "This kid loves Jesus" tee shirt, who get a cross tattoo ... you get the picture. But, Idleman says, Jesus didn't command his disciples to make "fans"; He sent them to build disciples—who, in Idleman's words, are followers who are completely committed to living their faith and advancing Jesus' mission—living it, 24/7. Completely. Committed.

IS that what a disciple is? Well, what can we find about this in the Bible?

- Jesus says in Matthew 10:38, "Whoever doesn't take up his cross and follow me doesn't deserve to be my disciple."
- He says in Luke 14:26-33, "If people come to me and are not ready to abandon their fathers, mothers, wives, children, brothers, and sisters, as well as their own lives, they cannot be my disciples. So those who do not carry their crosses and follow me cannot be my disciples.... In the same way, none of you can be my disciples unless you give up everything."
- When a wealthy official asks Jesus what he must do to inherit eternal life, Jesus quizzes him on Moses' Law and then advises him, "If you want to be perfect, sell what you own. Give the money

to the poor, and you will have treasure in heaven. Then follow me!" [i.e., become my disciple]....
When the official rejects Jesus' advice and goes away, Jesus says, "I can guarantee this truth: It will be hard for a rich person to enter the kingdom of heaven. I can guarantee again that it is easier for a camel to go through the eye of a needle than for a rich person to enter the kingdom of God." The disciples ask, "Then who can be saved?" Jesus answers that "It is impossible for people to save themselves, but everything is possible for God." Then Peter replies to him, "Look, we've given up everything to follow you. What will we get out of it?" (Matthew 19:16-27)

We see three things in this passage from Matthew: (1) when the official refuses to give up everything he has, he realizes he can't be Jesus' disciple; (2) Jesus affirms that wealth has nothing to do with salvation. Only God saves; and (3) according to Peter, being Jesus' disciples had indeed involved giving up everything.

It seems clear from passages such as these that Kyle Idleman is on the right track: being Jesus' disciple involves total commitment! God's Spirit calls each of us to whole-life discipleship—to be a follower of Jesus in every aspect of our lives. There's nothing "easy" about that calling to total dedication—but the Spirit *enables us to respond*.

Now … if *your* mission were to restore the kingdom of God—all of creation—beginning with the image of God in human beings, wouldn't you want totally committed people joining you in that project?

You're redeemed. Your whole self has been renewed for a relationship with God. The Holy Spirit is at work in you, enlightening you, teaching you, opening your eyes to the possibilities, opening your heart and mind to His call. He has enabled you to respond. So respond! No need to settle for being a *fan*, as Kyle Idleman might say. You can be a full-time disciple, joining God in His project of restoring His creation, beginning with the image of Himself in humans—in *you*. Every day, every way, from every angle and perspective: you can live life all-out—360 degrees—as a response to the Spirit's work in you.

D360. So what does 360-degree discipleship look like?

You will live out your whole-life response to the Holy Spirit's work in three primary contexts: (1) as an individual in an ever-growing, ever-deepening relationship with God; (2) as a part of the body of true believers around you and around the world—in perpetual community with God and with each other;

and (3) among non-believers—people who are not (or not yet) part of the Christian church.

Individual

We discussed earlier that, as human beings with a flawed nature and naturally rebellious souls, we do not have in ourselves the ability to believe that Jesus has bought us back into relationship with God by His death and resurrection. Our faith that this is a reality is born in each of us through the work of the Holy Spirit. Yet when that faith is born, your faith belongs to you, just as my faith belongs to me. Each of us owns his own faith; each of us responds in his or her own unique expression of revitalized spiritual living; each of us grows as an individual. Your living faith will be an intensely personal thing.

Much of your response to the work of the Holy Spirit will consist of things you yourself discover and integrate into your understanding as you grow in faith. But there will also be many things about your response to the Spirit's work that others teach you or that you learn from role models. Also, part of your response to the Spirit's work will be to lead, teach, and serve as a role model for other disciples. These are two reasons why growing as a disciple within a believing community—a larger part of the Body of Christ—is so important.

In the Body of Christ

I have devoted conversation Four to the ideal of
faith in community. Here in these two brief paragraphs I will lay the groundwork for that by point-
ing out simply that humans were created by God for
community—in fact, living in community together
with God and other believers is one attribute that
can most strongly reflect the image of God in us. It's
no accident that in his letters to the Romans, the Corinthians, the Ephesians and the Colossians, the
apostle Paul uses the metaphor "Body of Christ" to
describe the community of true believers—and no
metaphor does a better job of capturing the impor-
tance of relationships and community (although
Paul's related metaphor of marriage comes in a very
close second).

Many Christians first learn about God as part of a
community—typically their families. As I discussed
above, those who help build us into disciples
through teaching, coaching, mentoring, or modeling
are members of our community—whether a narrow
community such as our family or a broad community such as our church or the church of Jesus Christ
around the world. *And* each of us is called to fulfill a
role, or vocation, within the communities we belong
to; more on vocation in conversation Six.

Among Those Who Might Be Outside the Body of Christ

Perhaps at some point you have learned the term "best practice" (or "best practices"); if not yet, there's a good chance you will. A best practice is a "method or technique that has consistently shown results superior to those achieved with other means—and because of that is used as a benchmark."[3] Consider your life as a disciple of Jesus to be a "best practice" for daily living, whether you're around people who believe as you do or around people who have differing religious beliefs (or no religious beliefs). The disciple's ideals for learning, community, service, vocation, stewardship—even confession, forgiveness, healing and renewal—set a standard that others typically respect and often desire to emulate.

This is not to say that everyone will appreciate the outward witness of your "best practices." Jesus Himself advises us,

> If the world hates you, realize that it hated me before it hated you. If you had anything in common with the world, the world would love you as one of its own. But you don't have anything in common with the world. I chose you from the world, and that's why the world hates you.... If they persecuted me, they will also persecute you. (John 15:18-20)

But Jesus also encourages us,

> You are light for the world.... Let your light shine in front of people. Then they will see the good that you do and praise your Father in heaven. (Matthew 5:14, 16)

Your discipleship ideals—your *best practices*—are worth practicing, always, no matter whom you're with.

Summary

As a disciple of Jesus, you will live your faith as an individual, as a member of a believing community and as a member of the human family. Your faith is a gift, planted in you by God's Holy Spirit; your faith is your own, but your response to God's call to discipleship is the result of the Spirit's ongoing work in you. You will learn discipleship and pass it on as part of the fellowship of true believers in Jesus. As you go about your daily life, you will demonstrate your faith—sometimes among people who will not share your beliefs but who will often respect those beliefs and the way you live.

Deal With It

1. Some of the things author Rob Bell has written in recent years have become controversial among

Christ-followers, but he has always had a gift for asking questions that cause people to think deeply about faith. Setting aside any notions you might have about his more recent ideas for a bit, track down and watch his NOOMA video *Dust* (a pay-per-view version is available on YouTube's NOOMA Channel[4]). Share your thoughts about the relationship between disciples and their rabbis. Take some time to think and talk about it.

2. Describe the Holy Spirit's role(s) in disciple-building.

3. Is there such a thing as a casual or part-time commitment to being a disciple of Jesus Christ? Explain your response.

4. Billy Graham is often quoted as having said, "Salvation is free, but discipleship costs everything we have." Apart from the cost of total commitment of your life to Jesus and the restoration of His kingdom, what other costs might be associated with discipleship?

Go and Do

Think of someone in your family or in your church whose attitude of discipleship you would like to emulate in some way. What would you need to give up to follow his or her example? How would following his or her example change the way people perceive *your* attitude of discipleship?

Three
Christian Learning: Understanding God's Word

As a believer invited by God to work alongside Him in restoring His image in you and restoring His kingdom, His creation, you will have a deep desire to know God more—to have a greater sense of His immeasurable love for you, as well as a clearer, bigger understanding of His character and His plan to restore His kingdom. The Bible will be your primary source for learning these things.

Now, it's safe to say that there is confusion—maybe much confusion—about how to study the Bible for understanding. Perhaps what you understand from the Bible is rooted in catechetical study during which you memorized Scriptural "proof text" nuggets that support particular doctrinal teachings. Perhaps you have studied the Bible with a leader who has focused solely on the New Testament and who had no use for the Old Testament. Perhaps you have taken part in studies that presented a biblical book such as Revelation or the gospel of John or Ezekiel without connecting the ideas in them to the ideas in other biblical books. Perhaps you've attempted to read the Bible straight through from front to back.

Most of these methods have value at some level— but they all come up short if they do not help you understand how stuff in the Bible is connected to other stuff in the Bible—often a lot of other stuff. Here's an example:

> 18 The birth of Jesus Christ took place in this way. His mother Mary had been promised to Joseph in marriage. But before they were married, Mary realized that she was pregnant by the Holy Spirit. 19 Her husband Joseph was an honorable man and did not want to disgrace her publicly. So he decided to break the marriage agreement with her secretly.
>
> 20 Joseph had this in mind when an angel of the Lord appeared to him in a dream. The angel said to him, "Joseph, descendant of David, don't be afraid to take Mary as your wife. She is pregnant by the Holy Spirit. 21 She will give birth to a son, and you will name him Jesus [He Saves], because he will save his people from their sins." (Matthew 1:18-21)

Focus on verse 21, whose famous text reads, "She is pregnant by the Holy Spirit. She will give birth to a son, and you will name him Jesus [He Saves], because he will save his people from their sins." We know what this means, right? From the perspective of a literate 21st-century English-speaking Christian, it's no big deal to make this cognitive leap: "Ah, He was named Jesus because that name means 'Savior,'" or something like that. In fact, some translations—this one included—even help you make the leap, because they provide a handy note of some kind explaining that the name Jesus means "He saves" (or more often, "The LORD saves," which, as you will see, is more accurate).

But let's not make the leap. Let's actually look at what most people leap over:

1. Joseph of Nazareth was probably literate, but he was of course not a 21st-century English-speaking Christian. He was (probably) an Aramaic-speaking 1st-century Jew who knew his Hebrew Torah and the story of how the children of Israel got where they were; he knew, too, that God had promised an anointed Deliverer called the Messiah. But ...

2. Joseph had no reason to think that the Messiah should be named *Jesus*. In fact, the actual name "Jesus" as we know it would have meant nothing to him. However, the Hebrew name from which the English name Jesus is derived is *Yahoshua*.

And the name Yahoshua would have been tremendously significant to Joseph because ...

3. The name Yahoshua incorporated two very important things that speakers of Hebrew understood. The first is this: many generations earlier, Moses had chosen a young man named Hoshea to be his aide in leading the children of Israel. Hoshea's name meant "salvation" in Hebrew — but Moses changed his name to Yahoshua, which means "*Yahweh* is salvation" (Add the first part of Yahweh's name to Hoshea, apply a little Hebrew grammar, and you get Yahoshua. By the way, in our English Bibles, this man whom Moses renamed is called Joshua.). So Yahoshua, the name that the angel directed Joseph to give Mary's baby boy, meant "Yahweh is salvation." Unfortunately, this connection isn't easy to make — because of the second thing, which is that...

4. Most English versions of the Bible do not use the name Yahweh, the sacred name that God told Moses to call Him by in Exodus 3. Instead they opt to follow the traditional practice of substituting the word LORD (all uppercase) for Yahweh. So even a helpful note in your Bible that tells you Jesus' name means "The LORD saves" is not as helpful as it could be. The word "Jesus" never

meant "The LORD saves" in any language; it is merely a transliteration of the name Yahoshua (from Hebrew to Greek to Latin to English). But now we can see the significance of the angel's message: "You are to give him the name Jesus [that is, Yahoshua, which means 'Yahweh is salvation'], because he will save his people from their sins." See the assumptions that your translation might have made for you? You can't truly understand the meaning of this passage unless you also understand how stuff in the Bible is connected to other stuff in the Bible.

My advice (and it is so proverbial): look before you leap!

That is, read a passage and then ask "Am I sure I get what these words really mean?" Look for an overarching context; you might have to read a much larger chunk of Scripture than a verse or a section or even a chapter.

And, oh, does this mean that Jesus' name was actually Joshua? Well, yes, in a sense. A better way to understand His name is that He and the Joshua of the Torah and a priest named Jeshua (or Joshua in some translations), who is mentioned in the books of Ezra, Nehemiah and Zechariah, all had the name Yahoshua. It's likely that Jesus was called by a shortened form of Yahoshua—Yeshua.

It also means that although you may be accustomed to referring to Him as God or Lord, the God Who reveals Himself in the Bible has a name, an actual name, a *name* name: Yahweh[1]. See what He says about Himself in Exodus 3:4-16; most Bibles today still substitute LORD for the name Yahweh (a total of about 6,800 times, in fact). Are you interested in discovering what passages from the Old Testament look like with the name Yahweh restored? Find a "sacred name" version such as the Names of God Bible[2] (Read the Psalms especially; the difference is striking).

Look for big ideas

I used to drive past a billboard advertising a local church; it read, "At our church, the Bible is studied verse by verse." At first, that may sound like a good thing. But think again. Why would you study the Bible verse by verse? It wasn't *written* with verse divisions in mind. Verses are a relatively new development in Bible production (the first verse divisions were added in the 1480s by a rabbi named Isaac Nathan). A better way to think about the inspired composition of biblical books is that they were built idea by idea, or even theme by theme—and some of those ideas and themes are pretty big. What this means for you and me is that it's important to develop a sense for biblical ideas and themes. And often that will lead you into reading whole chapters as you study these ideas and themes—or even more.

Think about the persons named in a biblical passage, as well as about the listeners or readers for whom it was probably intended; what might they have understood that you might not—and how might your understanding rooted in 2000 years of Christian teaching and tradition be different from theirs? How often do details that you read appear to establish the authenticity of the events being narrated (Think about the mention of the historical person Caesar Augustus in Luke 2, for example)?

DO trust your previous training in reading the Bible—but take nothing for granted beyond the realities that (1) what you're reading is God's Word and (2) what you're reading is true. Reading the Bible for understanding is that important.

Want some guidance? Use the "Big Ideas in the Bible" list in the back of this book.

A Translation That Works

There is too much at stake in Bible study to treat the discipline casually. When you get serious about tackling the Bible, use a translation that you can trust to help you get the most out of what you read. Get one that is the product of sound biblical scholarship, but also be sure that the language is accessible—that

it makes sense when you read it. The language style
of the Bible you use need not be highly formalized—
that is, "fancy"; the language style most people used
two or three or four thousand years ago was no fan-
cier than the style you use every day. You may wish
to sample different translations on a multi-version
website such as biblegateway.com or studylight.org
or youversion.com; you may also wish to consult bi-
blegateway.com's section, "Picking the best Bible
translation for you." Don't be afraid to explore.

Should you use a translation or a paraphrase?
Keep in mind that a paraphrase such as The Living
Bible or *The Story* is a *re-telling* of the Bible's content
by one or more interpreters, while a translation is
typically the best attempt by a scholar or group of
scholars to render the actual inspired Word of God
from Hebrew, Aramaic and Greek into a non-biblical
language such as English. Whether you use a paraphrase version or not, I encourage you to adopt a true
and solid translation as a regular study resource.

Study! It's work, but it's great

Here are some suggestions to help you deepen
your study of the Bible:

• Study together with one or more other believers.
  Agree to be open to what you discover as you

study. Agree to treat disagreement as an opportunity for deeper study—and don't be afraid to consult a more experienced believer in matters of disagreement or uncertainty.

- The Bible reflects the intent of the Author (i.e., God; see 2 Timothy 3:16) and the writers He inspired. Always keep that in mind as you read the Bible. How *you* respond *personally* to a particular passage is secondary to this.

- Commentaries, study Bibles and other study resources can be helpful, especially for shedding light on difficult words and passages. It's healthy to remember, however, that most reflect a particular theological bias. From time to time you can learn almost as much simply by comparing several different English translations as you would searching for the meaning in a commentary.

- Find a mentor—a pastor, ministry leader, parent or experienced layperson—with whom to discuss what you learn as you study. The best mentors are patient listeners and thoughtful guides.

- When you study with a group or a mentor, don't be afraid to ask questions or challenge assumptions. Agree with your study partners that challenging long-held assumptions does not spring from a weak faith but from a thirst for deeper understanding. If you ask questions and challenge assumptions, you are in good company; read Acts 17:10-11 and see how the believers at Berea were admired for comparing what Paul taught them with Scripture.

- Consider a reading plan. There are many Bible-reading plans available from Christian publishers (and you can find others online—for free!); most will provide you a broad perspective and offer helpful guidance. Do some comparison-shopping before settling on a particular plan. If you try a plan that goes in a different direction than you expect, don't bail out right away; consider whether you could use it as a dummy "opponent" in an intellectual exercise to affirm what you believe.

- Pray. Invite God to send His Spirit to lead and enlighten you. Don't be afraid to wrestle with God in prayer when you go through rough spots in your study (God is a wrestler, after all. See Genesis 32).

Summary

As a disciple, you will desire to learn and understand God's plan for redeeming and restoring His kingdom. Your source for this understanding is the

Bible; it is God's story of His relationship with humanity, told through the inspired human writers of its 66 books. Understanding how to read the Bible—especially understanding how stuff in it is connected to other stuff in it—is almost as important as reading it is. When you get serious about digging into Scripture, be sure to get a Bible translation that will serve as the best tool for the job—one that faithfully renders the source languages (Hebrew, Aramaic and Greek) into English that makes sense to you. Nobody said studying the Bible would be easy—but the benefits are worth it.

Deal With It

1. What have you learned about God's work in the Old Testament, or the life of Jesus Christ, or the beginnings of the early Christian church, from actually reading about these things in the Bible (as opposed to hearing about them, for instance, in Sunday school)? Did anything you learned surprise you?

2. How do you know the Bible is true? What kinds of things help you trust the truth in its message?

3. Gaining an understanding of the message of the Bible has sometimes been compared to the party game known as Telephone—that is, some people

believe that the Bible's message changed, a little or a lot, when it was translated from Hebrew into Greek, and again when it was translated from Hebrew and Greek into Latin, and then from Hebrew and Greek into German (with Latin as an influence) and into English (with German and Latin as influences). How can a disciple of Jesus respond to this attitude?

Go and Do

Join—or start—a Bible study group committed to the guidelines offered in the "Study! It's work, but it's great" section of this chapter. For six months, keep a journal of (1) what you learn from the Bible and (2) what you learn about studying in a group like this.

Resources

- *GodConnects* from Lutheran Hour Ministries (www.lhm.org/godconnects)
- The Bible Project (www.jointhebibleproject.com)
- Video Bible Studies from Lutheran Hour Ministries (www.lhm.org/men/studies.asp)
- *Basic* from Flannel
- *For the Life of the World* from Flannel

Four

Community: God, You and Others

It was the plan from the very beginning: you were created for relationship.

Think about it.

One of the greatest mysteries we wrestle with about God is His trinitarian nature. How can He be both *one* and *three*? Many Christian teachers use the expression "three Whos but one What" to describe the one God Who is three Persons, Father, Son and Holy Spirit. One essence, three persons—one What, three Whos.[1] That's a helpful explanation, but if it doesn't solve the mystery for you, don't let that discourage you; even with such a handy phrase around, the fact that God is both three and one will remain a mystery to us all until we meet Him face to face (faces?).

Mysterious as it is, the inescapable truth as we find it in the Bible is this: God tells us that He exists in perfect, intimate community. God is Father, Son and Holy Spirit—one God but three distinct persons, living together in harmonious eternal community.

When He made humans in His own image, did that include building *us* to be in relationship, in community, with Him and with each other? Check out some of what the Bible says…

About the marriage relationship

Genesis 2:18-24

> 18 Then the LORD God said, "It is not good for the man to be alone. I will make a helper who is right for him."... 21 So the LORD God caused him to fall into a deep sleep. While the man was sleeping, the LORD God took out one of the man's ribs and closed up the flesh at that place. 22 Then the LORD God formed a woman from the rib that he had taken from the man. He brought her to the man.
>
> 23 The man said, "This is now bone of my bones and flesh of my flesh. She will be named woman because she was taken from man." 24That is why a man will leave his father and mother and will be united with his wife, and they will become one flesh.

Ephesians 5:25-33

> Husbands, love your wives as Christ loved the

church and gave his life for it. He did this to make the church holy by cleansing it, washing it using water along with spoken words. Then he could present it to himself as a glorious church, without any kind of stain or wrinkle—holy and without faults. So husbands must love their wives as they love their own bodies. A man who loves his wife loves himself. No one ever hated his own body. Instead, he feeds and takes care of it, as Christ takes care of the church. We are parts of his body. That's why a man will leave his father and mother and be united with his wife, and the two will be one. This is a great mystery. (I'm talking about Christ's relationship to the church.) But every husband must love his wife as he loves himself, and wives should respect their husbands.

About family relationships

Ephesians 6:1-4

Children, obey your parents because you are Christians. This is the right thing to do. "Honor your father and mother that everything may go well for you, and you may have a long life on earth." This is an important commandment with a promise.

Fathers, don't make your children bitter about life. Instead, bring them up in Christian discipline and instruction.

Colossians 3:18-21

> Wives, place yourselves under your husbands' authority. This is appropriate behavior for the Lord's people. Husbands, love your wives, and don't be harsh with them. Children, always obey your parents. This is pleasing to the Lord. Fathers, don't make your children resentful, or they will become discouraged.

About relationships with other believers

Psalm 133

> See how good and pleasant it is when brothers and sisters live together in harmony! It is like fine, scented oil on the head, running down the beard —down Aaron's beard—running over the collar of his robes. It is like dew on Mount Hermon, dew which comes down on Zion's mountains. That is where the LORD promised the blessing of eternal life.

1 Corinthians 12:12-27

> [T]he body is one unit and yet has many parts. As all the parts form one body, so it is with Christ. By one Spirit we were all baptized into one body. Whether we are Jewish or Greek, slave or free, God gave all of us one Spirit to drink.

As you know, the human body is not made up of only one part, but of many parts.... God's purpose was that the body should not be divided but rather that all of its parts should feel the same concern for each other. If one part of the body suffers, all the other parts share its suffering. If one part is praised, all the others share in its happiness.

You are Christ's body and each of you is an individual part of it.

About your relationship with God

Psalm 63

O God, you are my God.
  At dawn I search for you.
    My soul thirsts for you.
    My body longs for you in a dry, parched land
      where there is no water.
So I look for you in the holy place
  to see your power and your glory.
My lips will praise you
  because your mercy is better than life itself.
So I will thank you as long as I live.
  I will lift up my hands to pray in your name.
You satisfy my soul with the richest foods.
  My mouth will sing your praise with joyful lips.
As I lie on my bed, I remember you.
  Through the long hours of the night, I think about you.

You have been my help.
In the shadow of your wings, I sing joyfully.
My soul clings to you.
Your right hand supports me.

Other Psalms about relationship with God: 27, 38, 73, 119, 139

John 15:5-10

> I am the vine. You are the branches. Those who live in me while I live in them will produce a lot of fruit. But you can't produce anything without me. Whoever doesn't live in me is thrown away like a branch and dries up. Branches like this are gathered, thrown into a fire, and burned. If you live in me and what I say lives in you, then ask for anything you want, and it will be yours. You give glory to my Father when you produce a lot of fruit and therefore show that you are my disciples.
>
> I have loved you the same way the Father has loved me. So live in my love. If you obey my commandments, you will live in my love.

Romans 8:14-17

> For those who are led by the Spirit of God are the children of God. The Spirit you received does not

make you slaves, so that you live in fear again; rather, the Spirit you received brought about your adoption to sonship. And by him we cry, "Abba, Father." The Spirit himself testifies with our spirit that we are God's children. Now if we are children, then we are heirs—heirs of God and co-heirs with Christ, if indeed we share in his sufferings in order that we may also share in his glory.

Would you agree that in the Bible God promotes healthy, close and growing relationships? If God created us in His image, and one of his defining characteristics is perfect, eternal community, it makes sense that we would seek to be in community with Him and with others.

What this means for disciples of Jesus

God calls us into an ever-growing relationship with Him. He sends His Holy Spirit to lead us in developing it. In our conversations together, we will see a variety of ways in which this comes about—from study of His Word to worship to prayer, and more.

Faith Community: The Body of Christ

Our faith does not exist in a bubble. It is influenced and encouraged through the community we have with other believers—whether on a small and intimate scale (family) or on a larger scale (Bible study groups, ministry groups, the whole congregation). As we have seen in the passages above, the apostle Paul calls the community of believers the "Body of Christ"—a powerful image to describe just how deep and strong our relationships within the church could and should be as we respond together to Jesus' call to disciple people of all nations.

Disciples learn from other disciples; they learn by watching and listening to and emulating other disciples; they receive strength and encouragement and insight from disciples who have the benefit of knowledge and experience. Disciples hold each other accountable and teach each other repentance and forgiveness (more on this below). Disciples work together to pursue the church's mission.

Someone might challenge this and insist that he or she can believe in God and have a relationship with Him without membership in a church. And he or she is not entirely wrong. But belief and individual relationship with God aren't really the issues here—responding to the Holy Spirit's work of restoring the image of God in you is; developing fully as a committed follower of Jesus is; joining Jesus in His work of discipling all nations is. Christian community is the launch pad for all of these.

Marriage Community

In Genesis 1, we see a pattern emerge in verses 10, 12, 18, 21, 25 and 31: one after another, God pronounces the things He creates to be *good*; in fact, in verse 31, He looks across His entire creation and declares it to be *very* good (in Hebrew: *tov me'od*). But as we discover in the passage from Genesis 2 quoted above, God does identify something as "not good" (v. 18): "Then the LORD God said, 'It is not good for the man to be alone.'" And He declares immediately that He will remedy the situation: "I will make a helper who is right for him."

When God introduces to Adam the woman He has fashioned from Adam's rib, Adam knows intuitively how important this relationship is to be. "She's like part of me!" he seems to say, and maybe we can sense the wonder in his tone:

> This is now bone of my bones and flesh of my flesh. She will be named woman because she was taken from man.

In case we have missed what Adam is saying, the narrator of Genesis points us to a fundamental truth (v. 24): "That is why a man will leave his father and mother and will be united with his wife, and they will become one flesh." Recall from Genesis 1 that humans together are God's special creation (v. 27): "So God created humans in his image. In the image of God he created them. He created them male and female." Is it too great a stretch to suggest that the special marriage relationship—special community—between a man and a woman is a reflection of the image of Himself in which God created humans?

Well, consider one more thing. In the passage I've quoted above from Ephesians 5, Paul compares the love of husbands and wives to Jesus' love for the church: husbands are to love their wives as Christ loves His church and gave Himself up for her. He goes on,

> A man who loves his wife loves himself. No one ever hated his own body. Instead, he feeds and takes care of it, as Christ takes care of the church. We are parts of his body. That's why a man will leave his father and mother and be united with his wife, and the two will be one. (Ephesians 5:28b-31)

Christ the perfect image of God ... husband the likeness of Christ ... male and female created in the likeness of God ... husband united with his wife ... one body.... For Paul, how all these things are related is a mystery—and yet no less a reality: the community formed by the marriage of a man and a woman is rooted in the image of God in which humans were created. Paul even points back to the Genesis passage to make sure his readers make the connection.

Confession, Forgiveness, Healing and Renewal

Let's begin this section with four biblical passages. First, these two:

> The LORD is the only God. Love the LORD your God with all your heart, with all your soul, and with all your strength. (Deuteronomy 6:4-5)

> [L]ove your neighbor as you love yourself. I am the LORD. (Leviticus 19:18b)

Now these two:

> If we say, "We aren't sinful" we are deceiving ourselves, and the truth is not in us. God is faithful and reliable. If we confess our sins, he forgives them and cleanses us from everything we've done wrong. If we say, "We have never sinned," we turn God into a liar and his Word is not in us. (1 John 1:8-10)

> If any of you are having trouble, pray. If you are happy, sing psalms. If you are sick, call for the church leaders. Have them pray for you and anoint you with olive oil in the name of the Lord.

(Prayers offered in faith will save those who are sick, and the Lord will cure them.) If you have sinned, you will be forgiven. So admit your sins to each other, and pray for each other so that you will be healed.

Prayers offered by those who have God's approval are effective. (James 5:13-18)

So, what am I doing here—reviewing some of the Sunday school memory work you've had over the years? No (although reviewing Scripture passages you've memorized is never a bad thing). Or am I presenting the reasons why a section about confession, forgiveness, healing and renewal appears in a chapter about relationships? Yes.

Here are a couple of questions for you to consider: We often say that when we are together in a relationship, sin can separate us; let's turn the idea around: can there be sin where there is no relationship? Can there be *forgiveness* where there is no relationship?

What I'm trying to get at is this: there are two essential types of relationship in human existence, and these four passages point to what those are. One type of relationship is our relationship with God; whether the relationship is good or not so good or you don't know how to characterize it or you don't even know it's there, you and God have a relationship of *some* kind. The other type is our relationship with other humans. In the first pair of passages we see what God's standard is when it comes to relationships: He expects us to love Him above everything else; and He expects us to love our neighbors as we love ourselves. In other words, the bar is set pretty high.

We constantly fail to reach that bar—and this is what the second pair of passages is about. We routinely damage or even break our relationships with God and with each other. That's how sin works—it happens in relationships; it happens *because of* relationships.

So that's why the topic of confession, forgiveness, healing, and renewal is in this conversation about relationship and community.

As the passages in the second pair demonstrate, when my relationship with God or with a fellow human being is damaged by some wrong I have committed or by my failure to do some good thing that my fellow human being needs, then that relationship is in need of healing, restoration, and renewal. Healing and restoration begin with forgiveness; and forgiveness begins when I confess what I've done or failed to do.

The bottom line is this: God will not put up with our rejection of His will and direction; likewise, many of our relationships with others cannot withstand our poor treatment of each other. Confessing what we've done to harm someone else and seeking forgiveness are essential to restoring healthy community.

Additional passages about confession and restoration:

Leviticus 26:41-45

> If [my people] humble their uncircumcised hearts
> and accept their guilt, I will remember my prom-
> ise to Jacob, Isaac, and Abraham. I will also re-
> member the land. The land, abandoned by them,
> will enjoy its time to honor the LORD while it lies
> deserted without them. They must accept their guilt
> because they rejected my rules and looked at my
> laws with disgust. Even when they are in the land
> of their enemies, I will not reject them or look at
> them with disgust. I will not reject or cancel my
> promise to them, because I am the LORD their God.
> But for their sake, I will remember the promise to
> their ancestors. I brought them out of Egypt to be
> their God while nations looked on. I am the LORD."

Psalm 32:1-5

> Blessed is the person whose disobedience is forgiven
> and whose sin is pardoned.
> Blessed is the person whom the LORD no longer
> accuses of sin
> and who has no deceitful thoughts.
> When I kept silent about my sins,
> my bones began to weaken because of my
> groaning all day long.

Day and night your hand laid heavily on me.
My strength shriveled in the summer heat. Selah
I made my sins known to you, and I did not cover
up my guilt.
I decided to confess them to you, O LORD.
Then you forgave all my sins.

Proverbs 28:13

Whoever covers over his sins does not prosper.
Whoever confesses and abandons them receives
compassion.

Deal With It

1. How important to God are human relationships
and community?

2. We can experience community on many levels
within the church—in the larger body; in small
groups; in our own Christian family; in a mentoring relationship. Talk about the influence that
one or more of these types of relationship have
had on your growth as a disciple of Jesus.

3. See 1 Corinthians 12:27 and Romans 12:4-8. Talk
about Paul's metaphor that describes all believers
together as the Body of Christ. What does Paul's

use of this metaphor say about the image of God, unity and community, and our role in the restoration of God's kingdom?

4. It's normal for Christ-followers to develop relationships with people who do not confess Jesus as their Savior and Lord. How might this fit into God's plan for humanity—and for you in particular? How can you benefit from knowing someone who doesn't share your beliefs? How can that person benefit from knowing you?

5. How important to relationships are confession and forgiveness?

Go and Do

Proverbs 27:17 advises us, "As iron sharpens iron, so one person sharpens the wits of another." (Or, in another translation, "Just as iron sharpens iron, a person sharpens the character of his friend," CJB[2]) How could you be the iron that helps sharpen a friend's character? What would be your first (or next) step? Take that step.

Five

Prayer: Your Direct Access to the God Who Listens

Question: Where is prayer in the Bible? Answer: All over the place!

Check it out:

- Genesis 18. Abraham asks God to reconsider destroying Sodom.
- Genesis 20:17. Abraham prays to God on behalf of Abimelech.
- Exodus 8:9. Moses offers to pray for Pharaoh.
- 1 Samuel 1. Hannah prays for a son.
- 1 Kings 8. Solomon prays at the dedication of the Temple.
- 2 Kings 20. Hezekiah prays to Yahweh for healing.
- Psalms. Many of the Psalms are prayers.
- Ezra 10. The priest Ezra prays on behalf of the people of Israel.

- Job 42. Job prays for his friends.
- Daniel 6. Daniel prays three times a day.
- Daniel 9. Daniel prays a long prayer of confession, repentance and rededication on behalf of the people of Judah in captivity.

Isaiah prays; Jeremiah prays; Jonah prays from inside a fish; Ezekiel prays; Malachi prays; Jesus prays; Stephen prays; Paul prays. You get the idea.

Read Luke 11:1-4. Here's something to think about: with a 1,500 year-long heritage of their ancestors going to God regularly in prayer, why did Jesus' disciples feel the need to ask Jesus to teach them to pray? This passage and the corresponding passage in Matthew (Matt. 6:5-18) may offer some clues.

Luke reports, "Once Jesus was praying in a certain place. When he stopped praying, one of his disciples said to him, 'Lord, teach us to pray as John taught his disciples.'

"Jesus told them, 'When you pray, say this: Father....'"

Matthew's account adds some instructions about what not to do (vv. 5-9), including, "don't ramble like heathens who think they'll be heard if they talk a lot. Don't be like them. Your Father knows what you need before you ask him. *[Some translations warn against "vain repetition" rather than "rambling."]*

"This is how you should pray: Our Father in heaven…"

Getting back to our question about why the disciples asked for a lesson on prayer: are there clues about the disciples' motives in these accounts from Luke and Matthew? How about these:

- Jesus' disciples *observe* Him (probably actually hear Him) praying and desire to learn to pray as their rabbi prays—a reasonable request, since Jewish *talmidim* (i.e., disciples) expected their rabbi to teach them to do everything he could do. To reinforce their request, they point out that John the Baptizer taught his disciples to pray.

- Jesus advises that babbling, rambling, and repetitious praying spring from people's misguided assumption that God will be more apt to listen if they say a lot.

- The first thing Jesus teaches His disciples is to address God as "Father."

Can we learn something from these clues? Consider these inferences:

- When the disciples heard Jesus pray, did they perhaps recognize that His way of praying was different from (and superior to?) the way they had been taught to pray?

- Jesus warns against "rambling" or empty repetition. Apparently the disciples were aware of people of other religions who prayed that way (Greeks? Romans? Arabs or Persians? Perhaps.). Since Jesus points out that the pagans babble because they believe they'll be heard, it's safe to suppose He's referring to worthless prayers said to worthless gods who cannot hear, cannot know what we need (see v. 8), and cannot do anything in response.

- Jesus' instruction to call God "Father" in prayer is groundbreaking—revolutionary. Is Jesus teaching that God wants us to understand ourselves to be in a deep, trusting relationship with Him—as with a tender, loving Father? Yes, yes, yes.

Now think about this: be honest—have you ever caught yourself idly droning your way through the memorized prayer we know as the Lord's Prayer—the actual model that Jesus gave His disciples to teach them to pray? Why might that be true?

Let's look at something else. Have you ever wondered why, at a time when more than 450 English translations of the Bible have been published, Christians continue to pray the Lord's Prayer in the 400-year-old language of the 1611 Authorized (King James) Version? Why do you think this might be?

Well, can we just call it out here? It's easy to get comfortable, habituated (some might say "lazy," but I won't) in prayer. It's easy to get into a rut and mumble through a bunch of words we don't have to think about. But it is hard to use prayer as it was intended: as the way we communicate in deep, intimate relationship with the God Who loves us as a father—not just *a* father, but the best Father ever.

With God's help, we can change that.

First, let's be sure we understand what prayer is.

Talking to God ... speaking with God ... conversing with God ... "lifting up the heart and mind to God" (Martin Luther) ... pouring out our heart to God: these are some of the most-used ways of referring to the practice of prayer. In each we find three things: God, communication, and someone who is attempting to communicate (from now on referred to as "we/us").

Faith tells us that even though we often don't realize it, God is real and He is powerful and He is with us, and even though we don't see Him with our eyes, God pays attention to us every time we speak to Him. Read what John says at 1 John 5:14-15; what assurance does it give that God listens?

When it comes to communicating with God, we typically think of using language to do that—which is why we speak prayers, either out loud or in our thoughts, silently. It's also why Jesus warns against babbling. For the record, though, God is not bound by the limitations of human communication and hears even the prayers we have no language to express. Remember Matthew 6:5-18? Read it again, especially verses 7-8. Read Romans 8:26-27 also. What could this mean for your own prayer life?

Second, let's think about why we pray. From one commonly-held perspective, there are four reasons why we pray:

- God commands (or invites, or encourages) it;
- God has promised to hear and answer our prayers;
- God gave us prayers—even the very words of prayers—to say to Him;
- We have needs that we should be asking God to supply.

These are pretty inclusive, but we might add one. Look at Psalm 27:7-8:

> Hear, O LORD, when I cry aloud.
> Have pity on me, and answer me.
> {When you said,}
> "Seek my face,"
> my heart said to you,
> "O LORD, I will seek your face."

We have heard the phrase "seek God's face" and others like it often enough to think we understand them. But thinking we understand and actually understanding might not be the same thing. So let's take a close look at the expression. We can safely assume the phrase isn't literal but rather is a biblical figure of speech rooted in ancient Hebrew. The Hebrew word used here for "face" is *panim,* which is actually more accurately understood to be an abstract idea like "presence." So God invites us to seek—to desire—to be in His presence. The passage we just looked at parallels an earlier section (vv. 4-5) in the same Psalm, 27, which reads,

> I have asked one thing from the LORD.
> This I will seek:
> > to remain in the LORD's house all the days of my
> > life
> > in order to gaze at the LORD's beauty
> > and to search for an answer in his temple.

Being face-to-face with someone means you are close enough to look into each other's eyes and read each other's facial expressions. It means, too, there is no place to run to, no place to hide; each of you is open—transparent. Being in God's presence, truly being "face-to-face" with Him, involves this sort of closeness in spirit. To seek God's face is to desire to know Him deeply and intimately.

So, then, how do you seek God's face? Studying God's Word helps us to know Him better and can be a form of seeking His face. Participating in worship is another form of seeking God's face; worship focuses our recognition of the reality that we *are* in God's presence. And like worship, corporate prayer (i.e., prayer together with others, as in church) heightens our sense that God is present.

But in a spiritual way, it's *personal* prayer that is a one-on-one—face-to-face—encounter with God; and as with Bible study, if we carry on regular communication with God (i.e., if we pray often), we cannot help but get to know Him and His will better.

Read Psalm 139. Point out some of the Psalmist's thoughts that suggest he had sought (and found) God's face.

In prayer, just as in Bible study and worship, you have an opportunity to develop an ever-deeper relationship with God. You can tell Him what's on your mind; He will listen. You can ask for understanding; He will send you His Spirit to help you understand. You can gripe; He can take it. You can pour out your heart to Him; He will quiet you and rejoice over you with singing (cf. Zephaniah 3:17 NKJV[1]).

Now think about this. If regular communication with God helps us develop an ever-deeper relationship with Him, then whenever we invite a friend to pray for us, are we also inviting our friend to do something that could help deepen his or her relation-ship with God? Well, yes! If you are ever reluctant to ask someone to pray for you because you don't want to be a bother and foist your worries on someone else, think again; *it's an opportunity for ministry.*

Read the preceding paragraph again; it's impor-tant.

For further study: Read Psalms 32, 51, 63, 86, 102 and 119.

Tools to Guide You in Prayer

The Lord's Prayer

Okay, back to the Lord's Prayer for a bit. If you're someone who has gone through confirmation in-struction in the Lutheran Church (as I did), you have an acquaintance with Martin Luther's extensive teaching about this best-known and best-loved prayer, which, as we mention above, is found in Matthew 6 and Luke 11.

I won't re-invent Martin Luther's teaching on The Lord's Prayer.[2] Instead, I will mention an additional perspective about what we find in Scripture. In the English translations we use, there are some interest-ing differences between Luke's version of The Lord's Prayer and Matthew's. For one, Luke presents Jesus' teaching in a random place at a random time: "Once Jesus was praying in a certain place...." Matthew presents Jesus' teaching in the section of his gospel we call the Sermon on the Mount and launches into it without the narrative scenario that Luke uses: "When you pray, don't be like the hypocrites...."

A second difference is even more interesting. Luke reports, "Jesus told them, 'When you pray, *say this*: Father, let your name be kept holy....'" On the other hand, Matthew quotes Jesus as saying, "'*This is how you should pray*: Our Father in heaven, let your name be kept holy....'" That is, in one gospel, Jesus directs His followers to use the specific words He gives them, and in the other gospel, Jesus teaches them to use what He presents as a model for praying. There are more differences still, but this one is worth looking at closely—because it assures us of the freedom we enjoy in prayer.

Can both methods be valid—and complementary? For one thing, it is possible Jesus taught about prayer in this way more than once—perhaps to the twelve on one occasion and to a larger group on another. But also, as one scholar explains,

> [B]oth practices are good: We can pray prayers inspired by or adapted from Jesus' model prayer, and we can pray using the pattern of words he taught on either occasion. What is not good is the

empty chattering that can result from thoughtless recitation of a memorized prayer. Unfortunately, it seems likely that the Lord's Prayer is, of all the prayers of Christendom, the greatest martyr to thoughtless recitation.[3]

In other words, we need to understand that we have the freedom to use either method. The key is to grow closer to God as we pray.

So, do the 400-year-old words of the prayer from the Authorized Version, "Our Father, which art in heaven, hallowed be thy name ... Forgive us our debts as we forgive our debtors ..." afford you your best context for communicating with God, your loving Father? Then say those words.

Or do you find it more effective and fulfilling to construct a prayer that says the same thing, but in language of your own? Well, then, keep constructing prayers like that, perhaps using these ideas from Matthew as a guide:

> Our Father in heaven, let your name be kept holy. Let your kingdom come. Let your will be done on earth as it is done in heaven. Give us our daily bread today. Forgive us as we forgive others. Don't allow us to be tempted. Instead, rescue us from the evil one.

Jesus gave his disciples a tool, not a ball and chain; He taught freedom in prayer to our loving Father, not bondage to a rote ritual.

ACTS/ACTSS

Many teachers and mentors suggest using the acronym ACTS to help guide you during your prayer time. The letters in ACTS stand for different types of communication with God:

- **A = Adoration**: use of the language of worship and praise as you begin your conversation with your Creator and Lord
- **C = Confession**: that is, getting "on the same page" with God—first admitting to Him that you are guilty of rebelling against Him and rejecting His instructions and then asking Him to forgive you (which He is ready to do when you ask)
- **T = Thanksgiving**: that is, acknowledging God has given you everything good—and everything *for your good*
- **S = Supplication**: that is, asking your Creator, Savior, Lord and Provider for things you need (and things you want, too!)

Some add another S and make the acronym ACTSS. The extra S may refer to Surrender or Submission—that is, (1) the acknowledgment that God's will for you is always best and (2) the resolution that you are ready to accept His will even if you don't understand it.

Some suggest that the additional S might stand for Scripture; studying and praying passages from Scripture as you go can be a powerful supplement in communicating with God. For others, the extra S represents Song; for as long as people have followed Yahweh, some prayers have taken the form of song—and probably always will.

Finally, for some, the second S in the ACTSS acronym signifies Silence. Silence and prayer have gone hand in hand since ancient times. True silence is not easy to achieve! It's not just the absence of noise; it's the absence of anything that might distract you. Sometimes (and this can be the tough part), silence means not moving, not speaking, not even thinking, while God surrounds you with His presence. As with Surrender, Scripture and Song, Silence can often be a powerful weapon in the prayer warrior's arsenal.

Try the ACTS (or ACTSS) process from time to time; you may find it to be helpful as you grow closer to God in your prayer life.

Prayer Journaling

Many people find it helpful to write their prayers in a journal. Some leave a space after each prayer so that when they return and re-read the prayers they have written, they can record how they believe the prayer was answered. Your prayer journal doesn't have to be fancy—just helpful to your prayer life and to your development as a whole-life disciple of Jesus. Try journaling your prayers for a designated time— three months, six months, a year; see how God blesses you through it.

These are only a few tools you can use to guide you to a rich prayer life. What helps you grow closer to God through prayer? Share your ideas.

Praying in Jesus' Name

Clancy is a feature-length movie written, produced, and directed by Christian filmmaker Jefferson Moore. The movie's title character is an incredibly kind and gracious little girl who again and again forgives and prays for her abusive mother who is in a constant, losing battle against addiction.

Without fail, Clancy ends each prayer she utters with the same words: "It's in Jesus' name that I pray, Amen." Many of us have learned to close our prayers in the same way. But why?

The Bible says to do that, right? In John 14, for example, Jesus advises His disciples, "I will do whatever you ask in my name, so that the Father may be glorified in the Son" (John 14:13 NIV[4]). It seems self-evident from this that if I want Jesus to do something and end my prayer by saying, "I pray this in Jesus' name," then He will grant it, and the Father will be glorified.

But is that what the verse means?

Well, let's try a simple test. Have you ever asked for something, ended your prayer by saying "I ask this in Jesus' name"—and then NOT received what you asked for? It's safe to suggest that everyone has had at least ONE prayer that wasn't granted even though he or she ended the prayer with the tag, "In Jesus' name I pray."

Some well-meaning Christian friend might explain that not getting what you have prayed for using the "in Jesus' name" tag could mean that God has not responded with the answer "No" but with the answer "Wait." It's true that sometimes God's answer *is* "Wait." But imagine that someone has pled with God in this way to cure a loved one's fatal disease—and then the loved one has died. This isn't far-fetched; it happens, and the explanation that God has answered with "Wait" doesn't hold up, does it?[5] Perhaps you know someone who has given up praying—or even given up his or her faith—because a situation like this has shaken their trust in what they believe to be the Bible's promises. The following thoughts may be helpful.

The phrases "in my name" and "in Jesus' name" appear multiple times in the New Testament, so there are multiple alternate concepts of what it might mean to pray "in Jesus' name." We won't go through all of the possible interpretations; you can research them yourself on the Internet. But we will focus on one.

Think about some phrases that might begin with the words "in the name of." Here are a few that have come to my mind:

- In the name of freedom (or liberty)
- In the name of justice
- In the name of peace
- In the name of fairness
- In the name of mercy
- In the name of friendship

Now consider an example sentence: "She disagreed with his radical political views, but in the name of friendship, she kept silent."

Whenever the "in the name of" phrase is used in this way, it means "for the sake of" or "for the cause of." Now think about Jesus' command again and re-phrase it with that in mind: "I will do whatever you ask *for my cause,* so that the Father may be glorified in the Son."

First of all, what about that doesn't make sense? Answer: nothing. If what we ask for truly advances Jesus' cause—to redeem all of humanity, tell the Good News, show others how to become disciples, and restore His kingdom—why would we not expect Him to grant our prayer? And if it *doesn't truly advance that cause,* why would we be surprised if God's answer turns out to be "No"?

And second, could this mean that there might be no particularly good reason to tack the phrase "in Jesus' name" onto the end of our plea? If what we ask for truly advances Jesus' cause, will it not be granted whether we say the words or not?

Earlier you read 1 John 5:14-15; read it again with the following thought in mind. God is holy, perfectly just, good, merciful, all-knowing, all-wise—in fact, He is love itself. If we know this, if we are confident of this, what's the best thing we could possibly pray for? His good will and purpose for the world— which, ultimately, results in salvation and life forever with Him? Of course!

Could this mean that whether we say the words or not, we are praying "in Jesus' name" *every time we pray for God's will to be done?* Think about it.

Summary

Prayer is spiritual communication through which God can help you build a closer, deeper relationship with Him.

- Our communication with God typically makes use of language, but God is not bound by the constraints of human communication and knows what you need before you speak with Him about it in prayer.

- God invites everyone who believes in Him to pray to Him honestly and sincerely. God is not impressed with the babbling of many words or the mindless droning of memorized prayers. However, He is ready to hear honest prayers, even ones that are full of anger and frustration; He made us, and He can handle our anger and frustration.
- Learning what it means to "seek God's face" can be helpful in developing your prayer relationship with Him.
- Tools such as the Lord's Prayer and the ACTS/ACTSS acronym can serve as important guides as God leads you closer to Him through prayer.
- "Praying in Jesus' name" and ending your prayer with the words, "in Jesus' name" might not always mean the same thing.

Deal With It

1. Is prayer about asking for stuff? Explain.

2. The song "Audience of One," released in 2002 by the band Big Daddy Weave, is a deeply spiritual poem about prayer. It includes the lyrics, "I come

on my knees to lay down before You,/Bringing all that I am, longing only to know You,/Seeking Your face and not only Your hand,/I find You embracing me, just as I am." Talk about the possible meaning(s) of the line, "Seeking Your face and not only Your hand." Look at the whole song (see below). What language does songwriter Mike Weaver use to highlight prayer as something through which God draws us closer to Him?

3. What in your prayer life is helping you to grow closer to God?

4. Some people have misguided notions about the way we should pray. What practices or under-standings about prayer do you wonder about—have concerns about?

5. What keeps you from praying the way you want to?

Go and Do

Choose one of the tools mentioned above and in-corporate it into your prayer habits over a desig-nated period of time. Pay attention to the way it in-fluences what you pray about and how you pray.

Audience of One

I come on my knees to lay down before You,
Bringing all that I am, longing only to know You.
Seeking Your face and not only Your hand,
I find You embracing me, just as I am.

And I lift these songs to You, and You alone;
As I sing to You, in my praises make Your home.

To my audience of one: You are Father and You are Son;
As your Spirit flows free, let it find within me
A heart that beats to praise You.
And now just to know You more has become my great
reward.
To see Your kingdom come and Your will be done,
I only desire to be Yours, Lord.

So what could I bring to honor Your Majesty?
What song could I sing that would move the heart of
royalty,
When all that I have is this life that You've given me?
So Lord, let me live for You my song with humility.

And Lord, as the love song of my life is played,
I have one desire: to bring glory to Your name!

To my audience of one: You are Father and You are Son;
As your Spirit flows free, let it find within me
A heart that beats to praise You.

And now just to know You more has become my great
reward.
To see Your kingdom come and Your will be done,
I only desire to be Yours, Lord.

And we lift these songs to You, and You alone;
As we live for You, in our praises make Your home.

To my audience of one: You are Father and You are Son;
As your spirit flows free, let it find within me
A heart that beats to praise You
And now just to know You more has become my great
reward.
To see Your kingdom come and Your will be done
I only desire to be Yours, Lord.
Yours alone! You alone, yeah.

AUDIENCE OF ONE
Michael Weaver

Six

Worship: It Might Not Be What You Think. It's More.

Ask 50 people at your church the question, "What is worship?" and some, perhaps many, will respond that it's the time the congregation gathers on Sunday mornings to praise God, hear a message from His Word, celebrate the sacrament of communion and offer prayers as the Body of Christ. Search the Internet for the topic and you will come up with many articles and videos on worship with this as their focus. Well, even though there is little in the Bible to support these folks' perspective on worship, they're not wrong.

But worship deserves to be looked at from a broader perspective.

Here's a thumbnail of different forms that worship took in the Bible:

- Prior to the Exodus, there was no formal priest-hood, and people worshiped God in simple ways.

Cain and Abel brought sacrifices and offered them to God. When Noah came out of the ark, he built an altar and offered sacrifices to God. While living in Beersheba, Abraham took Isaac to a mountain nearby to bring a burnt offering to God.

- There were priests around, however. Abraham was blessed by Melchizedek, priest of El Elyon, God Most High (long before the family of Levi was chosen to be the priestly class in Israel—for that matter, long before there was such a thing as Israel). After fleeing from Egypt, Moses worked for the priest Jethro, also called Reuel, in Midian (and married his daughter). No accounts are available of what the duties of priests such as Melchizedek and Jethro entailed, although offering animal sacrifices was undoubtedly one of them.

- From very early on, prayer—by individuals, by groups, by priests on behalf of believers—was part of Old Testament people's life of worship, both formal and personal.

- When God re-established his covenant with Israel at Mount Sinai, the tribe of Levi was chosen to be Israel's priestly class. At first, the people worshiped Yahweh in the open at the foot of Mount Sinai. Then Yahweh commanded Moses to build a tent, or tabernacle, in which He would live among the Israelites wherever they went. Priests from the tribe of Levi cared for the tabernacle and performed ritual duties as Yahweh directed. When the Bible describes the worship practices of the Israelite people, it commonly depicts them as bowing down with their faces to the ground—a gesture of absolute submission and respect.

- King David was influential in making song an important part of worship-related activities. Many of his psalms also speak of dancing as an expression of worship; and David himself danced before Yahweh "with all his might" when the Ark of the Covenant was brought into Jerusalem after David took the city from the Jebusites.

- Plans to build a permanent dwelling place for Yahweh began under David and were undertaken and completed under his son Solomon. The Temple became the center of ceremonial worship for all of Israel. The priests continued their service of bringing sacrifices for sin and burnt gift offerings on the people's behalf.

- When the Temple was destroyed by the Babylonians in 586 B.C., people gathered for corporate praise, learning and prayer at synagogues in Jewish communities, both in Israel and in the countries of the diaspora. Scribes and sages served as the rabbis (teachers) who led these groups of Jews in their devotional activities.

- Weekly gatherings at the synagogue resulted in a shift in focus for the observance of the Sabbath. Even when the Temple was fully operational, it had not been possible for most Jews to go to the Temple every week for formal worship; so the traditional priority on the Sabbath had been rest. In synagogues, laypeople were permitted—and expected—to participate alongside rabbis. Synagogue worship services typically involved praise, prayers, Scripture readings, and a sermon or explanation of the reading. So synagogue worship became a much more active thing, although rest remained an important—and carefully monitored—component. The practice of gathering weekly in synagogues continued after the Temple was rebuilt—as well as after the destruction of the Second Temple by the Romans in A.D. 70.

- Glimpses of a life of worship in the first-century church run from Acts through the letters of Paul and beyond. Acts 2 offers a rich, if brief, picture of community around Jesus the Messiah; we see a group of believers developing a culture of fellow-

ship and joyful response to the work of the Holy
Spirit:

> The disciples were devoted to the teachings of the
> apostles, to fellowship, to the breaking of bread,
> and to prayer. A feeling of fear came over everyone
> as many amazing things and miraculous signs
> happened through the apostles. All the believers
> kept meeting together, and they shared everything
> with each other. (Acts 2:42-44)

But very little direction is offered in the New Testament about gathering for formal corporate worship. Paul's first letter to the church at Corinth
offers a basic outline:

> So what does this mean, brothers and sisters? When
> you gather, each person has a psalm, doctrine,
> revelation, another language, or an interpretation.
> Everything must be done to help each other grow.
> (1 Corinthians 14:26)

But if you go looking through the New Testament for detailed instructions in planning and
running the kind of structured order of worship
found in many churches today, you will not find
any. This may be due in part to an ancient understanding of the idea of worship that isn't common anymore. I'll unpack that next.

"Worth-ship?"

You can find a lot of sources that will explain to you that the word "worship" comes from an Old English word, *weorthscipe*, which evolved into "worth-ship," and eventually into "worship." You can infer what the general sense of it is: our worship is what we do to acknowledge the worth, or *worthiness*, of our God—our holy, all-powerful Creator, Preserver and Redeemer.

One challenge we have to deal with, though, is that "worship" is an English word that evolved from a word in a language that is no longer spoken (i.e., Old English, or Anglo Saxon), and that word was a translator's best attempt at rendering a Latin word (*adoro*) that was commonly used to translate two Hebrew words and two Greek words. Just explaining that is confusing. Does "worth-ship"—a term signifying our acknowledgment of God's worthiness— offer a full understanding of what those words conveyed in Hebrew and Greek?

Let's have a look.

The two Hebrew words are *shachah*—to bow low in humility, adoration and reverence, and *abad*—to serve.

The two Greek words are *proskuneo* (roughly equivalent to *shachah*) and *latria* (roughly equivalent to *abad*).

Now let's look more closely, beginning with the obvious.

The Obvious

When you bow (*shachah*), you bow in relation to something, right? When you adore or revere (*shachah*) or serve (*abad*), your behavior always has an object—the thing that receives your adoration or reverence or service. That *is* obvious, isn't it? Well, for believers, so is the identity of the object of our adoration or service: it's *God* Whom we adore, revere and serve.

How we know to do those things is only slightly less obvious: through our faith, God reveals Himself to us in His Word and His supernatural gifts for us —the sacraments of baptism and communion—and through the love and compassion of our fellow members in the Body of Christ, the true church. God teaches us that He is the One Who made us, the One Who loves us unconditionally, the One Who redeemed us from sin, the One to Whom we belong in faith, and the One Who sends us His Spirit to enlighten and inspire us and to equip us to serve.

When we desire to be in God's presence, when we adore or revere or serve Him, we are *responding* to Who God is, what He has done, and what He is doing. And maybe this is where the truth is less obvious for a lot of people:

Worship is our response to Who God is and what He's done for us.

No doubt if you go back through the examples we listed earlier from biblical history, you'll notice that that's one thing they all have in common: whether it was bowing in submission and reverence, participating in Temple worship, or performing acts of service, whatever behavior was considered worshipful in the Bible involved people responding to God for Who He was and what He had done.

But Wait...

If you are wrestling with some questions right now, that's good. Here are two that you might be kicking around:

- If worship is my response to the God Who has done so much for me and is transforming my life right now, wouldn't I want to be worshiping more than just an hour or two on Sunday?
- If worship is my response to God through adoration and reverence and service, wouldn't worship be diverse—couldn't it end up taking on as many forms as there are individuals in the world?

The answers to these questions are yes and yes. Let's explore further by surveying a few passages from Scripture (you knew this was coming, right?):

Worship: It Might Not Be What You Think. It's More.

Deuteronomy 6:4-9

Listen, Israel: the LORD is our God. The LORD is the only God. Love the LORD your God with all your heart, with all your soul, and with all your strength. Take to heart these words that I give you today. Repeat them to your children. Talk about them when you're at home or away, when you lie down or get up. Write them down, and tie them around your wrist, and wear them as headbands as a reminder. Write them on the doorframes of your houses and on your gates.

Nehemiah 8:5-6

Ezra, standing higher than all the other people, opened the book in front of all the people. As he opened it, all the people stood up. Ezra thanked the LORD, the great God. All the people responded, "Amen! Amen!" as they raised their hands and then bowed with their faces to the ground and worshiped the LORD.

Psalm 40:6b-10

You did not ask for burnt offerings or sacrifices
    for sin.
Then I said, "I have come!
    (It is written about me in the scroll of the book.)

I am happy to do your will, O my God."
Your teachings are deep within me.
I will announce the good news of righteousness
among those assembled for worship.
I will not close my lips.
You know that, O LORD.
I have not buried your righteousness deep in my heart.
I have been outspoken about your faithfulness
and your salvation.
I have not hidden your mercy and your truth
from those assembled for worship.

Psalm 50:7-15

"Listen, my people, and I will speak.
Listen, Israel, and I will testify against you:
I am God, your God!
I am not criticizing you for your sacrifices or burnt
offerings,
which are always in front of me.
But I will not accept another young bull from your
household
or a single male goat from your pens.
Every creature in the forest,
even the cattle on a thousand hills, is mine.
I know every bird in the mountains.
Everything that moves in the fields is mine.
If I were hungry, I would not tell you,
because the world and all that it contains are mine.
Do I eat the meat of bulls or drink the blood of goats?

Bring your thanks to God as a sacrifice,
   and keep your vows to the Most High.
Call on me in times of trouble.
   I will rescue you, and you will honor me."

Psalm 141:3

Doing what is right and fair
   is more acceptable to the LORD than offering a
   sacrifice.

Hosea 6:6

I want your loyalty, not your sacrifices.
I want you to know me, not to give me burnt offerings.

Micah 6:6-8

What should I bring when I come into the LORD's
   presence,
   when I bow in front of the God of heaven?
Should I bring him year-old calves as burnt offerings?
Will the LORD be pleased with thousands of rams
   or with endless streams of olive oil?
Should I give him my firstborn child because of my
   rebellious acts?
Should I give him my young child for my sin?
You mortals, the LORD has told you what is good.
   This is what the LORD requires from you:

to do what is right,
to love mercy,
and to live humbly with your God.

Luke 2:36-37

Anna, a prophet, was also there. She was a descendant of Phanuel from the tribe of Asher. She was now very old. Her husband had died seven years after they were married, and she had been a widow for 84 years. Anna never left the temple courtyard but worshiped day and night by fasting and praying.

John 4:23-24

… The time is coming, and it is now here, when the true worshipers will worship the Father in spirit and truth. The Father is looking for people like that to worship him. God is a spirit. Those who worship him must worship in spirit and truth.

Acts 2:44-46

All the believers kept meeting together, and they shared everything with each other. From time to time, they sold their property and other possessions and distributed the money to anyone who needed it. The believers had a single purpose and went to the temple every day. They were joyful

and humble as they ate at each other's homes and
shared their food.

Romans 12:1-2

Brothers and sisters, in view of all we have just
shared about God's compassion, I encourage you to
offer your bodies as living sacrifices, dedicated to
God and pleasing to him. This kind of worship is
appropriate for you. Don't become like the people of
this world. Instead, change the way you think. Then
you will always be able to determine what God
really wants—what is good, pleasing, and perfect.

1 Corinthians 6:19-20

Don't you know that your body is a temple that
belongs to the Holy Spirit? The Holy Spirit, whom
you received from God, lives in you. You don't
belong to yourselves. You were bought for a price.
So bring glory to God in the way you use your body.

1 Corinthians 10:31

...whether you eat or drink, or whatever you do,
do everything to the glory of God.

1 Corinthians 14:26b

Everything must be done to help each other grow.

Ephesians 5:16-20

Make the most of your opportunities because these are evil days. So don't be foolish, but understand what the Lord wants. Don't get drunk on wine, which leads to wild living. Instead, be filled with the Spirit by reciting psalms, hymns, and spiritual songs for your own good. Sing and make music to the Lord with your hearts. Always thank God the Father for everything in the name of our Lord Jesus Christ.

Colossians 3:12-17

As holy people whom God has chosen and loved, be sympathetic, kind, humble, gentle, and patient. Put up with each other, and forgive each other if anyone has a complaint. Forgive as the Lord forgave you. Above all, be loving. This ties everything together perfectly. Also, let Christ's peace control you. God has called you into this peace by bringing you into one body. Be thankful. Let Christ's word with all its wisdom and richness live in you. Use psalms, hymns, and spiritual songs to teach and instruct yourselves about God's kindness. Sing to God in your hearts. Everything you say or do should be done in the name of the Lord Jesus, giving thanks to God the Father through him.

Hebrews 10:24-25

> [L]et us consider how we may spur one another
> on toward love and good deeds, not giving up
> meeting together, as some are in the habit of do-
> ing, but encouraging one another—and all the
> more as you see the Day approaching.

Hebrews 13:15-16

> Through Jesus we should always bring God a sac-
> rifice of praise, that is, words that acknowledge
> him. Don't forget to do good things for others and
> to share what you have with them. These are the
> kinds of sacrifices that please God.

1 Peter 2:9

> [Y]ou are chosen people, a royal priesthood, a holy
> nation, people who belong to God. You were cho-
> sen to tell about the excellent qualities of God, who
> called you out of darkness into his marvelous light.

That's a lot of Scripture—but then, worship is a
big topic, and my hope is that this array of passages
is helpful to your understanding of that. In addition
to sacrifice, submission, praise, adoration and reverence, did you also see the following concepts at work
in these passages?

Toward God

- Love
- Dedication, obedience, and loyalty
- Prayer
- Inward sincerity (as opposed to outward show)
- Thankfulness
- Trust and reliance
- Offering what you are and what you have
- Openness to the Holy Spirit's influence
- Honesty with yourself and with God

Toward others

- Love
- Sharing your faith openly with others
- Teaching your faith to your family/loved ones
- Kindness, mercy and compassion
- Humility
- Forgiveness
- Harmony
- Equity
- Encouragement and support
- Setting a good example
- Honesty with each other

The list of passages and characteristics of worship could be longer still, but the important thing for all of us in this little exercise is to acknowledge that worship is a *whole-life response* to God for Who He is and what He does for us. One writer describes this whole-life response in similar terms:

> Worship is the response of the whole being—heart, soul, mind, strength—to beholding God's glory. It is enabled by the Holy Spirit. (There is no worship apart from spiritual regeneration.) It is fixated on gospel truth. (We behold God's glory in the face of Jesus Christ.) It is directed by God's self-revealing Word. (We don't intuitively figure out what pleases God.) It involves personal and corporate expressions. (We worship in all of life as well as in church gatherings.)[1]

Made right with God entirely as a free gift from Him alone, we are daily renewed and enabled to respond to the work of God's Spirit in us. He invites us to live sanctified—holy, *restored*—lives, and when we respond in faith, worship results. And in this sense— in the sense that it's our Spirit-fueled response to Who God is and what He does—worship is truly what the Old English word *weorthscipe* meant: declaring the *worth*, or *worthiness*, of God.

So what does worship look like? In light of what we've learned, our worshipful response to God is colorful and rich and diverse. It could look like this:

Toward God

- Active prayer life—including praying for and with other believers
- Intentional study of God's Word
- Offering your natural gifts and talents to support corporate worship and other activities in your faith community
- Participation in the worship gatherings of your faith community (i.e., "going to church")
- Giving of financial gifts for God to use according to His purposes
- Regular family and personal devotion/meditation time
- Confession of sin and the assurance of forgiveness, restoration and renewal
- Caring for your body as a temple of the Holy Spirit

Now take a moment to think: do you see how this list of responses is related to the image of God idea that we have explored in preceding chapters? Here are some thoughts:

- When you are active in prayer or corporate worship or family or personal devotions, you are accepting God's invitation to be in community with Him.
- When you study God's Word, you are responding to His call to seek to know Him, His mind and His

will—and to have Him mold Your life as He intends.
- When you confess the things you've done to damage your relationship with God or with someone else, you acknowledge that the image in which humans were created, His image, is flawed in you—and that only He can restore His image in you to what it was meant to be.
- When you care for your body, develop and use your personal gifts or offer your time, talent and treasures in Jesus' name, you are responding to God's work of sanctification—and reflecting back to Him the restored, renewed, sanctified image with which Jesus has covered you. Not only that, but you are also joining Him in his project of restoring His creation.

In service to others

- Educating other Christians—children and adults—in the faith
- Modeling an attitude of faith and trust in God
- Sharing your faith with non-believing family members, friends and neighbors
- Offering your natural gifts and talents to relieve suffering and encourage others who are struggling
- Developing your natural gifts and talents and using them to help and encourage your business and community

- Using your influence for the good of others in your community
- Being a wise and compassionate parent of your children and/or a respectful and obedient child of your parents
- Bringing up children in the Christian faith
- Participation in service projects

Interestingly, the concept of worshiping by serving others dovetails with the teaching on Christian *vocation*. In a nutshell, the teaching explains that God has created everyone with a variety of gifts and talents to serve others in a variety of ways—often very ordinary ways. A person's vocation is God-given, and his or her response to the work of the Holy Spirit is to embrace that vocation and perform it to the best of his or her ability.[2]

You're probably coming up with other aspects of what worship can look like. The point that I don't want you to miss is summed up in two of the passages above: "Love the LORD your God with all your heart, with all your soul, and with all your strength" (Deuteronomy 6:5) and "Whether you eat or drink, or whatever you do, do everything to the glory of God" (1 Corinthians 10:31). Devotion of heart, soul, and strength—everything you are and everything you do—for God's glory: worship is a big thing; it's a response thing; it's a life thing.

Well, but...

By this point in the chapter it would be fair for you to be wrestling with this question:

> In another chapter *discipleship* is described as 360-degree whole-life response to the work of the Holy Spirit. Now you're saying *worship* is a whole-life response to the work of the Holy Spirit. Which is it?

Well, you'll notice that I placed the concept of worship *within* the concept of discipleship, and that's one good way of looking at it. If you're living your life—360 degrees, your whole life—as a disciple of Jesus, there's no way for constant worship *not* to be a part of that. But the truth is that prayer, offering, service, Bible study, and building Christian community are elements *both* of whole-life worship *and* whole-life discipleship. So the two "-ships" are inextricably connected to each other, and neither fits neatly into its own compartment in our lives.

However, there are some distinctions to be discovered in the different focuses of our discipleship and worship activities. Am I the focus? For example, do I study the Bible to understand God and grow in faith— that is, to try to become a stronger follower of Jesus? Then *discipleship* is my emphasis and my worship is indirect. Or is God the focus? For example, do I come to church and sing "Hallelujah!" (which means "Praise Yahweh!") and offer my gifts to God because of His goodness and love? Then *worship* is my emphasis and it is direct. Does it matter? In the grand scheme of faith, no. Whole-life worship is integral to whole-life discipleship ... *and* whole-life discipleship is integral to whole-life worship. It's never a question of *which*. Later we will even explore one more "-ship" to which God calls disciples of Jesus to respond with their whole lives.

Corporate Worship

The worship activity that most people recognize is corporate worship—when we set aside a special time and gather together as a family, or body, of believers. When we respond to God by gathering with others in corporate worship, we make God the sole focus of our activity—whether we are singing praise, listening to His Word, giving our offerings in sincere thanksgiving, confessing the faith we share, or celebrating communion together. God gives us everything good; we give Him thanks, praise and our own simple gifts in return.

And, as a matter of fact, what happens in corporate worship is never "one-way": that is, while our gathering together is to focus solely on God for Who He is and what He does, He also offers gifts to us: His powerful Word, His Holy Spirit, His body and

Worship: It Might Not Be What You Think. It's More.

blood in the sacrament of communion, and the assurance of forgiveness, restoration and renewal.

Additionally, corporate worship offers us the opportunity to interact in a special way. Recall that when God created humans in His image, He created us for *community*; He created us to be together—both with each other and with Him. Interestingly, the term "corporate" has its roots in the Latin word "corpus" —that is, *body*. In corporate worship, believers worship together as one—acting as a body does. As we've seen, Paul compares all believers to a body in Romans 12, 1 Corinthians 12, and Ephesians 4. We are Christ's body, and when we worship as His body, He builds us up, strengthens us, and encourages us through His gifts and through each other. The writer of the Hebrews 10 passage quoted in the Scripture section above affirms this; here it is again:

> [L]et us consider how we may spur one another on toward love and good deeds, not giving up meeting together, as some are in the habit of doing, but encouraging one another—and all the more as you see the Day approaching.

Finally, when we confess our faith together, we join in spirit with all the believers around us and all who have ever made the same confession[3]. When we pray together, we are all communicating with God

Himself. And when we celebrate communion together, we are united with God and with each other in a unique spiritual relationship.

In corporate worship we have the potential to come as close as we ever will during our lives to encountering what God intended for His relationship with His highest and most beloved creation—human beings, whom He created in His own image.

Personal devotional activities

Somehow, without Bible apps, devotional apps, catechism apps, prayer apps and praise song apps on their smartphones (well, without smartphones, for that matter)—in fact, without even Bibles or devotional books in their hands or in their homes— people in the Bible appear to have had a rich devotional life. Consider Moses' advice to the Children of Israel in Deuteronomy, which I quoted earlier in this chapter:

> Love the LORD your God with all your heart, with all your soul, and with all your strength. Take to heart these words that I give you today. Repeat them to your children. Talk about them when you're at home or away, when you lie down or get up. Write them down, and tie them around your wrist, and wear them as headbands as a re-

minder. Write them on the doorframes of your houses and on your gates. (Deuteronomy 6:5-9)

Not only did the Israelites grow up learning the teachings of the Torah by heart; they also taught their children by way of a constant dialogue about what God's Word and will meant for their lives.

The Bible gives special recognition to private worship practices—especially including the following:

- King David's life of personal devotion: "Oh, how I love your teachings! They are in my thoughts all day long" (Psalm 119:97).
- Daniel's daily prayer habit (Daniel 6:10)
- The prophetess Anna's constant worship at the temple (Luke 2:36-37)
- Jesus' retreats to secluded places for prayer (Mark 1:35).
- The devotional life of Timothy's family, which we glimpse when Paul writes, "[C]ontinue in what you have learned and found to be true. You know who your teachers were. From infancy you have known the Holy Scriptures" (2 Timothy 3:14-15).
- Paul and Silas' private worship time in an unexpected place: prison (Acts 16:25)

Personal and family devotional times that include Bible reading, a brief message, prayer, and even singing and other components (creeds, catechism recitations and more!) do in a far more intimate way what corporate worship does on a mass scale. Alone or in your family circle, private worship offers you special opportunities to respond to Who God is and what He does with adoration, praise and prayer; special opportunities to learn from Him; special opportunities to feel His presence and sense the forgiveness, restoration and renewal He offers through Jesus.

The best time and place for a personal or family devotional time are what are best for you. Morning is a great time—but so is the time just before you turn out the light at night. Around the table or the fireplace, on a walk or bike ride, in a chapel or in full view of a sunrise, *where* doesn't matter nearly as much as who is there: you, together with the God Who made you in His image and Who loves to spend time with His children.

Summary

Our worship is the outpouring of our Spirit-guided response to God for Who He is and what He does. The Bible characterizes worship as a lifelong, 24/7 thing—a constant attitude of thanksgiving and praise that acknowledges God for his power and goodness. The Bible demonstrates that God is big on sincerity, not show. Regular participation in corporate worship provides us the opportunity to offer gifts to God and receive gifts from Him; it also fosters the unique interaction, or communion, among God, the body of believers, and the individual. Participation in corporate worship strengthens each of us and equips us to serve others. The practices of personal and family worship (devotion) are responses to God that offer special opportunities for God to build a deeper relationship with us and to deepen the spiritual bond among the members of our family.

Deal With It

1. What does whole-life worship look like for you — how do YOU respond *worshipfully* to God's love and power in your life?

2. It's not unusual for someone to have an aversion to worship because he or she had a negative reaction to a corporate worship experience: "It's so boring"; "I don't like the hymns"; "I don't like the contemporary songs"; "I'll never get the whole chanting thing"; "why do we have to sit so still and just listen to the speaker?" And so on. What ideas from this chapter could you share with a person who has misconceptions about worship because of his or her negative experience?

3. No doubt you've heard somebody say this: "I don't need to go to church to be a Christian" or "I don't need to be a part of a church to live my faith." Is the person who says this right? If not, why not? If so, what advice could you offer this person?

4. Martin Luther famously wrote that the parent who changed his or her baby's diapers and the dairy worker who milked cows were doing holy work because they were responding to God by serving their neighbors. Discuss how this idea is related to worship. How do *you* "worship" by serving others in ordinary ways?

5. *"Our church worships about 500 people every Sunday."* Professional church workers hear things like this from time to time. Call it churchspeak; it's shorthand for the expression, "About 500 people attend worship at our church every week." But if you looked at it and thought "Well, about 500 people *worship ONE God at MY church every week*," then you exposed one of the flaws in its use of the verb "worship." Talk about the relationship of the worshipers with the One being worshiped—and why it might be wise to avoid using the term "worship" in this way.

Go and Do

Use a Psalm today as the basis for a brief personal devotion. Repeat this practice for a month, using different Psalms and exploring different themes.

Seven
Stewardship: It's NOT (All) About Money?

Let's just say it: it seems that more often than not today, when a church uses the term "stewardship," it's talking about money. Right? In some places, the Sunday when the pastor preaches about tithing, offerings and annual financial pledges is called Stewardship Sunday. There are "stewardship" Bible studies that are all about financial management. If you Google "Christian stewardship," many of your results will link you to sites that talk about careful financial management, first-fruits giving, priority-percentage giving, cheerful giving ... you get the idea.

Well, as you no doubt recognized, that was the setup. Here's the payoff: although money is involved, stewardship is not all about money. It's not mostly about money. It's not halfway about money.

Stewardship is about why humans were created. And why Jesus came and died and rose. So don't let people's tendency to focus on money distract you from the reality that stewardship is ... (wait for it) ... *a much bigger deal than we might've been led to assume.*

A (really) big picture

Let's build the idea of stewardship, using thoughts I've already presented in other chapters, together with related biblical details that may not have entered into our conversation yet:

1. Humans are the pinnacle of God's creation. He created humans "in His image"—uniquely imbued with features of His own character. And He gave them the choice of living in a harmonious relationship with Him through obedience and trust—or living apart from Him through rebellion and rejection.

2. God placed humans in a garden, blessed them, and told them, "Be fertile, increase in number, fill the earth, and be its master. Rule the fish in the sea, the birds in the sky, and all the animals that crawl on the earth."

3. Long after the creation of humans—and, significantly, long after humans rebelled against God—David writes in Psalm 8,

> When I look at your heavens, the creation of your
> fingers,
>> the moon and the stars that you have set in
>> place—
>> what is a mortal that you remember him,
>> or the Son of Man that you take care of him?
> You have made him a little lower than yourself.
> You have crowned him with glory and honor.
> You have made him rule what your hands
>> created.
> You have put everything under his control:
>> all the sheep and cattle, the wild animals, the birds,
>> the fish,
>> whatever swims in the currents of the seas.

In passages like these we get a glimpse of God's purpose for His creative masterpiece, human beings: He created humans to work with Him—to be His managers, His *stewards*—in ruling over, caring for and enjoying His entire creation. All of His creation. All that His creation would become. Forever. *Stewardship* was God's original purpose for us.

4. But humans made an unfortunate choice: they rejected God's terms. Ever since, the image of God in humans has been imperfect, corrupt, enfeebled, mortal. Humans are helpless to fix this.

5. However, God never stopped loving His creation—any part of it. Once, as I have mentioned, He was so fed up with the evil to which humans had sunk that He destroyed all but eight people. But He never gave up entirely, and in fact He put in motion a plan—the only plan possible—to restore the relationship He craves with His creation, by first restoring the image of Himself in humans and then working with humans to restore the rest of His creation. He set about *pursuing* us, beginning with Noah and then Abraham. Ultimately, He sent His Son among humans to be both God and human; to live the obedient life that humans were incapable of; to die in the place of every human ever and atone for the rebellion of every human ever; and to come back from death to life to seal the victory and restore every human who believes in Him.

What a picture of love. Think for a moment about that passage we all know, "For God so loved the world that he gave his one and only Son, that whoever believes in him shall not perish but have eternal life" (John 3:16 NIV). How many people pay almost no attention to the little word "so" in this teaching of Jesus? And yet what it's there for is to point to the absolutely astonishing extent of God's love for the humans who rejected Him. God loved His creation *so*

fiercely, so recklessly, so much, so crazy-much, that
He sacrificed His Son to restore His relationship
with us—to win back His creative masterpiece.

6. We read in 2 Corinthians 5:17-20 that through the
   power of the Holy Spirit, we are brought to the
   faith which believes that we are restored to God
   through the life, death and resurrection of Jesus,
   God's only Son. God invites us back into a holy
   relationship with Him through which we will be
   restored to our role as His co-workers and caretakers of His creation, both on this earth and the
   new earth to come. That new earth is described
   here:

   > I saw a new heaven and a new earth, because the
   > first heaven and earth had disappeared and the
   > sea was gone. Then I saw the holy city, New
   > Jerusalem coming down from God out of heaven,
   > dressed like a bride ready for her husband. I
   > heard a loud voice from the throne say, "God lives
   > with humans! God will make his home with them,
   > and they will be his people. God himself will be
   > with them and be their God." (Revelation 21:1-3)

7. When faith opens our eyes to this, we respond—
   in whole-life worship; as whole-life followers
   (disciples) of Jesus, our Teacher, Redeemer, and

King; *and* as whole-life stewards of everything—
Every. Thing.—that God gives us.

So that's what I'm suggesting when I say that
stewardship is not (all) about money. It's a far bigger
thing. And like discipleship and worship, stewardship is a whole-life-response kind of thing.

In an earlier chapter I introduced a thought by
author Gabe Lyons in his book *The Next Christians:
Seven Ways You Can Live the Gospel and Restore the
World.* Let's look at his extended thought in the context of stewardship as I have presented it here:

> The next Christians believe that Christ's death and
> Resurrection were not only meant to save people
> *from* something. He wanted to save Christians *to*
> something. God longs to restore his image in
> them, and let them loose, freeing them to pursue
> his original dreams for the entire world. Here,
> now, today, tomorrow. They no longer feel bound
> to wait for heaven or spend all of their time telling
> people what they should believe. Instead, they are
> participating with God in his restoration project
> for the whole world.[1]

Lyons isn't the first person to paint a picture of
our stewardship that looks like this. His idea is a
twenty-first-century echo of one of the apostle Paul's

teachings for the believers at Ephesus:

> God saved you through faith as an act of kind-
> ness. You had nothing to do with it. Being saved is
> a gift from God. It's not the result of anything
> you've done, so no one can brag about it. God has
> made us what we are. He has created us in Christ
> Jesus to live lives filled with good works that he
> has prepared for us to do. (Ephesians 2:8-10)

Believers are new creations in God's grace, called to
the ministry of restoration—a ministry of doing
good in the world and helping others meet the God
Who has restored us to Himself.

So what does this whole-life response of stewardship look like; what has God called us to be stewards of?

- **Life**. God calls us to be faithful managers of all
  living things. Animals and plants have been provided for food, clothing and other aspects of human life, and we are called to use them conscien-
  tiously and humanely. Human life is worth protecting and preserving—at every stage of life, in
  every circumstance—and this includes looking
  out for people's health and well-being. And as
  God's co-workers in the restoration of humanity
  to Himself (see 1 Corinthians 3:9), we are *also* to
  be stewards—keepers, protectors, sharers—of his

message to humankind, the Gospel (see Ephesians 3:2-11), so that everyone has the opportunity to come to the knowledge of God's truth (see 1 Timothy 2:1-6).

- **The world we live in.** As with animals and plants, God has given us non-living natural resources—solar energy, air and wind, water, minerals, soil and landforms, and so on—to use for our good and the good of our fellow human beings. God made and owns and cares for all of it (see Psalm 24:1-2 and Psalm 95:3-7). God calls us to work alongside Him and to emulate Him in his care for the non-living treasures of His creation.

- **Time.** Scripture doesn't skimp when it comes to teaching God's people about the stewardship of their time. In one place we find David praying, "Teach us to number our days so that we may grow in wisdom" (Psalm 90:12); in another we see Paul advising, "[Make] the best use of the time, because the days are evil" (Ephesians 5:16); elsewhere we hear James haranguing, "You don't know what will happen tomorrow. What is life? You are a mist that is seen for a moment and then disappears" (James 4:14). And this is just a tiny sample. Maybe Paul offers the best exhortation for stewardship of time to the church at Corinth:

> Since we are God's coworkers, we urge you not to let God's kindness be wasted on you. God says, "At the right time I heard you. On the day of salvation I helped you." Listen, now is God's acceptable time! Now is the day of salvation! (2 Corinthians 6:1-2).

Note Paul's urgency. What was true in the first century is true for us today: the time we have is short, and there are many people who are not yet disciples of Jesus—many whose time will run out before they can receive God's grace through faith. Now *is* God's acceptable time.

- **Gifts, talents, abilities**. As I mentioned earlier in our brief discussion about Christian vocation, God has made each of us unique—each crafted in His image but equipped with a vast diversity of gifts, talents and abilities. And He has called us to develop those things for good—especially the good of our fellow disciples and others. Jesus was serious about God's special personalized gifts to us; read what He says in what has come to be called the parable of the talents, Matthew 25:14-30. The apostle Paul talks about the value of individual gifts, talents and abilities in his teaching on the church as the Body of Christ, which I have mentioned in previous chapters; read again what he says about the use of our gifts in Romans 12, 1 Corinthians 12, and Ephesians 4.

Everything you can do is worth using to serve the church and others. And it's worth doing well. Check the parable of the talents again; God is looking forward to saying to you, "Good job! You're a good and faithful servant!"

- **Knowledge and Technology.** It's no secret that we live in an age when information and technology are the engines by which much of the world moves. Our mobile devices literally put more knowledge at our fingertips than ever before—more information than we know what to do with. Knowledge, information, learning, data... whatever you call it, much of it is neither inherently good nor inherently bad—but it can be used to hurt as well as to help. Our job is to handle knowledge wisely and discreetly, always seeking to help, to build up, to connect people to the source of good for their lives—Jesus.

  Knowledge is paired with wisdom throughout the Bible. Search the term "knowledge" in the so-called Books of Wisdom—Job, Psalms and Proverbs—and note all the passages that compare and contrast knowledge/wisdom with ignorance/foolishness. Here's a great proverb to keep in mind: "The one who has knowledge uses

words with restraint, and whoever has understanding is even-tempered" (Proverbs 17:27).

- **Possessions and finances**. So *now, at last,* we get
  to money and what God teaches us about it and
  about our possessions. Earlier in this chapter I
  pointed you to a passage in Psalm 24; here's the
  first verse from it: "The earth and everything it
  contains are the LORD's. The world and all who
  live in it are his" (Psalm 24:1). Sermons about financial stewardship often use this passage to
  teach that since everything we have belongs to
  God, nothing we have belongs to us; rather, it's
  all a trust from God, and He expects us to manage it carefully. The parable of the talents in Matthew 24 teaches us the same thing. The unavoid-
  able truth is that we DO have possessions and we
  DO have money, both of which ARE gifts from
  God. God calls us to act wisely as we acquire and
  use them—to act in accordance with our character as His co-workers, created *and re-created* in His
  image to join Him in His project to restore His
  creation.

  Sermons about financial stewardship often
  also remind us that since everything belongs to
  God, we have a responsibility to offer some of it
  back to Him in grateful (and, of course, cheerful)
  response. And this is where, for some reason, the

idea of stewardship can become a bit distorted. Alvin Barry, who served as president of The Lutheran Church—Missouri Synod from 1992 to 2001, once wrote,

> Unfortunately, at times when stewardship is discussed it is done from the perspective of the Law, not the Gospel. In fact, it may well be that a number of people think that stewardship is only about raising funds for the church's budget.[2]

Our motivation to give should not come from the Law[3]; nor should it be driven by the need to pay the church's bills. This is why I made such a big deal in the preceding conversation about connecting giving to *worship*. It's important not to confuse financial stewardship with the financial gifts we offer in worshipful response to God. The two *are* connected; wise financial practices such as budgeting, saving, living within your means, and careful investing can help free you truly to *worship* God with your money.

What this means is that in much the same way as discipleship and worship are related, so are stewardship and worship related. Whole-life stewardship is interconnected with whole-life worship; and whole-life stewardship *supports* worship activities—in particular, (1) your reverence and care for other humans and for all of God's creation; (2) your development and use of your gifts and abilities; and (3) your habits of worshiping God with your money and possessions.

So stewardship truly is not (all) about money. It's about discipleship, and it's about worship. Ultimately, it's about God's purpose for you as a unique creation fashioned in His image.

Summary

Christian stewardship is about so much more than money. When God created humans, He made them *stewards*—managers, caretakers—over the rest of His creation. His original plan was for them to work alongside Him in overseeing His good kingdom; after humans broke His covenant with them, His plan involved restoring not only His image in them but also restoring humans to the role for which they were intended. Our wise and faithful management of life and health; the world we live in; knowledge and technology; and our time, gifts, talents, abilities, money and possessions acknowledges God as the Creator, Ruler and Giver of everything; *and* it demonstrates the Holy Spirit's ongoing restorative work in us.

Deal With It

1. Read Psalm 104. How does the psalm writer characterize God as Creator? What is the relationship of all creatures to their Creator? According to what you have read in Psalm 8, where do humans fit into God's big picture?

2. Read Colossians 1:13-20. What is the relationship of God's Son, Jesus Christ, to the world God created? What's His relationship to humans in particular?

3. What does being a good steward mean to you?

4. You are the pinnacle of God's creation and imbued with the very image of your Creator—so *creativity* is part of your makeup. Do you consider yourself creative? How does exercising your creativity reflect faithful stewardship?

5. Financial stewardship: talk about it. Go ahead; you can handle it.

Go and Do

Research an organization such as Save the Storks, Care Net, Lutherans Restoring Creation, or Voice of the Martyrs. As a disciple called to be a faithful steward of creation, including human life and health, learn what involvement in the organization's work might mean to you, to the lives of individuals and families, and to that organization's community. Or choose another organization, such as Birthright, End Slavery Now; Loose Change to Loosen Chains; Open Doors International, Blessed Earth, etc.

Eight
Disciple-building. And Witness. And Evangelism.

So. Discipleship is a 360-degree whole-life response to the Holy Spirit's work to restore the Kingdom of God, beginning with God's image in you. I'm pretty sure you have figured the next thing out already, but I'll say it anyway—for emphasis....

Jesus has a special command for all of His disciples: *"Join me in making more."*

Yes! As a committed follower of Jesus with a desire to be close to Him, to be like Him, to live in harmony with His mission, each of His disciples will dedicate his or her life to discipling others.

Now, there is an expression that warns, simply, "The devil is in the details." Any concept can sound like a good idea *at the conceptual level*, but many of them fall by the wayside when we encounter the often thorny details of putting the concept into practice.

Discipling others everywhere *does* sound like a great idea. And why not? It's Jesus Himself Who calls us to this task. But *how* to help people become disciples is where we often find ourselves paralyzed. We balk as we imagine starting *that* conversation and the ways people could find to shut us down:

"Are you saved?" *"What do I need to be saved from? I'm fine; no salvation required today, thanks."*

"If you were to die tonight, where would you end up?" *"It won't matter to me; I'll be dead."*

"I'd like to introduce you to a friend of mine; His name is Jesus." *"The last thing I need is a new friend—I don't care who he is."*

"Repent!" *"You go first."*

"Would you like to come to church with me?" *"Churches are full of hypocrites; anyway, I attend the 'church of my choice.'"*

"God has a message for you: He loves you." *"Who—that invisible guy in the sky? Let Him come stand here and tell me Himself."*

Any of those sound familiar? And there's no truly good way to argue around some of those scary attitudes effectively, is there? After all, they're not spoken to invite conversation; they're spoken to bring your conversation to as abrupt an end as possible.

Well, let's stop there for a moment and have a

look at what Jesus said in what has become known
as the Great Commission passage, Matthew 28:18-20
(NIV):

> "All authority in heaven and on earth has been
> given to me. Therefore go and make disciples of
> all nations, baptizing them in the name of the Fa-
> ther and of the Son and of the Holy Spirit, and
> teaching them to obey everything I have com-
> manded you."

Just about any seminary student will jump at the
opportunity to share with you that this rendering
doesn't accurately translate the sense of the language
of its Greek source. In the Greek, there is only one
imperative verb (command); it is neither "Go" nor
"make"; it's this: "disciple." That is, "help someone
else develop into a disciple." The Greek language in
the gospel of Matthew doesn't imply that you need
to "*make* disciples." Why is that important? It takes
the pressure off of you to *produce a disciple* and simply invites you into the *Holy Spirit's process of disciple-
making*!

Our seminary-student friend would also point
out that while most people learned that Jesus said
"Go," the sense of the Greek word used in Matthew,
poreuthentes, is, as I mentioned, not the imperative
"Go!"—but rather the participial "Going" or "Having

gone." Why is this important? From this it appears that Jesus wasn't necessarily saying "Go someplace *else* and do this"; rather, He was instructing his disciples to disciple as they were "going," "wherever you go," "whenever you go" — that is, while you are doing what you do in the course of your life. Some modern translations of Matthew attempt to reflect these grammatical distinctions, but not many succeed.

So, then, Jesus calls us, His disciples, to *disciple* others in all the circumstances of our lives. Does this mean that we have opportunities to disciple in:

- our relationship with a friend at work? Yes.
- our relationship with our fiancé/fiancée or spouse? Yes.
- our relationships with our children? Yes.
- our relationship with a college roommate? A college acquaintance? A college professor? Yes. Yes. Yes.
- our relationship with our neighbor across the street? Yes.
- our relationships with our fellow believers? Yes.
- our relationships with people in other parts of the world who have never heard of Jesus? Yes.
- our relationships with people who disagree with us on social or political (or even religious) issues? Yes!

Disciple-building. And Witness. And Evangelism.

This is a very diverse list of scenarios, isn't it? But no doubt you have not missed why I've grouped them together: discipling typically happens within relationships. Some thought leaders go so far as to say that discipleship is always *caught* rather than *taught*—and of course the best way for discipleship to be caught is in the context of a relationship.

I believe that last claim is worth qualifying, though. In John 8 Jesus is speaking with some people identified as "Jews who believed in Him"; He advises them, "If you live by what I say, you are truly my disciples. You will know the truth, and the truth will set you free." One way to look at this is that it's possible for the discipling process to happen *outside* a relationship with another human being. We can learn to be disciples by learning what Jesus has to teach us and then living according to it through the Holy Spirit's guidance.

But a discipling *relationship* is more common— and often more efficient. In just a bit we'll unpack a couple of the scenarios we've listed above, but before we do, I want to introduce a concept you might not have given a lot of thought to.

Missiologist Alan Hirsch points out that while Jesus' disciples were without a doubt *disciples*, they might not have been converts—that is, true believers in Jesus as God's Son and the Messiah—until late in their relationship with Him.[1] Think about it:

- Although chronology in the gospels is sometimes tricky, it's apparent that by the 4th chapter of Mark, the disciples have been following Jesus for a time, but after He calms the sea, He says, "Why are you such cowards? Don't you have any faith yet?" and Mark says that the disciples "were overcome with fear and asked each other, 'Who is this man? Even the wind and the sea obey him!'"

- The first true confession of faith by any of the disciples occurs more than halfway through Matthew (chapter 16): "Who do you say that I am?" Jesus asks them; "You are the Messiah, the Son of the living God!" Peter answers. It's true that John reports in the second chapter of his gospel that after the miracle with water and wine in Cana, "his disciples believed in him" (v. 11); yet this does not specify *what* they believed about Jesus. If someone you know tells you, "I believe in you," what does that mean besides "I believe I can trust what you do and what you say about yourself"? The statement in John may be no more than that. On the other hand, Peter's declaration in Matthew leaves no room for alternative interpretations; it's a creed that declares exactly Who he believes Jesus is.

What Alan Hirsch asserts is this: Jesus was undoubtedly discipling these twelve guys (and others) for some time before they were true believers that He was the Messiah and the Son of God. Disciples first, believers second, in Jesus' and the Holy Spirit's own time.

Not quite an interpretation you're accustomed to? But interesting, maybe?

All right; let's look at some discipling scenarios.

Child

Christian parents *disciple* their children — they tell them stories from the Bible; they teach them songs that express belief in rudimentary ways; they teach them to pray simple prayers; they model the walk of a disciple of Jesus. As the child develops, the Christian parent continues to teach him or her more complex, deeper truths about God and His plan to restore humanity. Does the parent wait to do this discipling until the child has professed his or her faith? No; the parent simply disciples. As the parent speaks and lives the Gospel in his or her child's life, the Holy Spirit works in the child's heart and soul to foster a living, growing faith.[2]

Fellow believer — lunch and discipling

Picture this conversation between two Christian guys:

"Whoa, I really appreciated that Bible study-hour session; money management according to biblical principles—I've never looked at finances that way before."

"I'm still processing—not sure I'm making sense of it all."

"It was a lot to take in—and that was just the first session. Hey, want to grab some lunch and compare notes?"

"Like I took notes."

"I mean review what the leader said and deal with the stuff we might not have understood. *Iron sharpens iron*, that sort of thing."

"Good; I really didn't want to have to take notes. Yeah, yeah—let's do that. What do you say: every week, after the study hour?"

"Sure; let's see what happens. And if notes need to be taken, I can do that. Let's not forget our Bibles."

"No probs, right? Dude, we both have Bible apps on our phones."

"That was a rhetorical remark for the people reading this."

"Oh, yeah, right. So, um, lunch: who's buying?"

"How about whoever doesn't take notes?"

And so begins a discipling relationship—each believer committing to help the other develop as a disciple of Jesus.

Girl in your dorm—free lunch and discipling

Imagine the following conversation:

"So are you going home this weekend?"

"Nah, I thought I'd just hang around here, maybe do some laundry if I feel like it. What're you doing?"

"There's a bunch of us getting together to go across town tomorrow morning and rake leaves for some elderly people."

"Why?"

"The campus ministry I'm involved in does this every fall.... Want to come?"

"Um, I don't usually do church stuff."

"Well, yeah, we'll probably have a prayer at the beginning and maybe even talk a little bit during the day about the activities our group does, but mostly we'll just be helping out some senior folks, just raking leaves and having a good time together. And there's a free lunch."

"Uh..."

"Oh, come on. *Lunch*—plus a chance to do something good for somebody... or *laundry*? Sounds like a no-brainer to me."

"Well, okay, I guess so. What could it hurt? But I might change my mind."

"No you won't."

"I might."

"No you won't."

This person has not moved an inch toward belief; she will not rake leaves on Saturday and come for baptism on Sunday. But her Christian friend can disciple her, can't she? She can demonstrate her Gospel-fueled desire to serve; she can model Christian compassion; she can strengthen her friendship with her schoolmate and find common interests and passions that they can build on; she can introduce her friend to others in her faith community; she can set the stage to take their conversation past laundry and raking leaves to more meaningful things. Sometimes the disciple-building process begins with slow and careful baby steps such as these.

A non-believing friend (lunch optional)

Imagine saying to a non-believing friend, "I'm studying what the Bible teaches about leadership (or wisdom or relationships or racism or slavery or parenting)—interested in joining me and having some discussions?"

It's likely, isn't it, that your friend might be put off if you were to ask, "If you were to die tonight, where do you think you will spend eternity?" But isn't it possible that an invitation like the one in the preceding paragraph might NOT put your friend off—and might even pique his or her curiosity? And if he or she were to say, "Eh, sure, what's the worst that could

happen?" ... you could disciple your friend—teach him
or her what it means to be a follower of Jesus—and do
so without strings, without any expectation that he or
she will pray some new believer's prayer, without any
threat of rejection. Your relationship could actually
grow stronger in this non-threatening context—and,
well, you could let the Gospel and the Holy Spirit
work on your friend through the experience (which is
as it should be; which is the only way it can be, really).

Witness and Evangelism

One thing I don't want to do is give the impres-
sion that discipling, as I've described it, has nothing
to do with witness and evangelism. As with so much
we've looked at in this series of conversations, these
ideas are interrelated. AND all three are important
for the disciple. So let's look at these two other
things—witness and evangelism—in order to clarify
how they all work together.

Witness

Jesus' expectation is that his followers will be witnesses. We can see this clearly in the first chapter of Acts:

> After his death Jesus showed the apostles a lot of
> convincing evidence that he was alive. For 40 days

he appeared to them and talked with them about God's kingdom.

4 Once, while he was meeting with them, he ordered them not to leave Jerusalem but to wait there for what the Father had promised. Jesus said to them, "I've told you what the Father promises: 5 John baptized with water, but in a few days you will be baptized with the Holy Spirit."

6 So when the apostles came together, they asked him, "Lord, is this the time when you're going to restore the kingdom to Israel?" 7 Jesus told them, "You don't need to know about times or periods that the Father has determined by his own authority. 8 But you will receive power when the Holy Spirit comes to you. Then you will be my witnesses to testify about me in Jerusalem, throughout Judea and Samaria, and to the ends of the earth." (Acts 1:3-11)

The verse that's probably most familiar to us is verse 8: "You will be my witnesses to testify about me in Jerusalem, throughout Judea and Samaria, and to the ends of the earth." What I have done is embed it in its context—verses 3-11. As you see, the verse is part of a "what next" conversation after Jesus has spent 40 days demonstrating over and over to his disciples that He is indeed alive. The conversation

Disciple-building. And Witness. And Evangelism.

develops in this way:

1. Jesus directs the disciples not to leave Jerusalem but to wait for something special.

2. The disciples infer that Jesus is about to do the Messiah thing that they have learned from tradition: He will take back the kingdom of Israel from Rome and restore it to the glory it had under David and Solomon. They ask Him if now is the time.

3. Jesus redirects their focus: "Wrong question," He implies when He tells them they don't need to know about times the Father has set…. "*But,*" He explains, you will receive power when the Holy Spirit comes to you … and (instead of kicking foreign invaders out of Israel) you will testify about me and my death and resurrection—both in Israel and out there, everywhere."

The word "witness" in our English Bibles translates the word *martys* or *martyria* in the Greek source documents. *Martys* signifies a person who can give accurate testimony about something; *martyria* signifies the testimony itself. You probably noticed that the Greek word *martyria* looks a lot like our English word "martyr." The original Christian martyrs were people committed to giving faithful testimony about

Who Jesus was and what this meant for everybody. Many also were persecuted and even executed because they stood by this testimony. The connotation stuck; in our minds the word "martyr" has more to do with losing your life for your faith than about simply testifying that what you believe is the truth.

In the Acts passage, Jesus uses the term *martys* to call His disciples to give reliable testimony. Paul tells the church at Corinth in 1 Corinthians 15, "I passed on to you the most important points of doctrine that I had received: Christ died to take away our sins as the Scriptures predicted. He was placed in a tomb. He was brought back to life on the third day as the Scriptures predicted." Earlier in the same letter he mentions that when he came to Corinth, this was the thing—the only thing—he was determined to do among them. This is His ideal, his witness, his *martyria*.

It can be our ideal today too—and it dovetails with the concept of Christian vocation much the way worship-driven service does (cf. conversation Six). That is, when our lives are guided by the simple truth, "Jesus died for me; He was buried; He rose from the dead to seal my redemption and call me to life with Him," we are testifying to Who Jesus is and what He means for everyone who believes; we are *being the witnesses he calls us to be* in Acts 1. This is true for wherever we are, and whatever we do—whether we are telling the story of Jesus' death and

Disciple-building. And Witness. And Evangelism.

resurrection or we are serving, building a relationship, sitting in class, earning a living, mowing the
lawn, changing a tire, going on a mission trip, going
hang gliding, going on vacation ... *whatever*.
So. We are called to disciple others everywhere
we go. And we are called to be witnesses of Jesus'
love in everything we do as we respond to the work
of the Holy Spirit in us. In whole-life discipleship?
Yes. In whole-life worship? Yes. In whole-life stewardship? Yes.

*Selected Bible passages related to witness: Ephesians
5:1-2; 1 Corinthians 11:1-2; Ephesians 2:8-10; 1 Timothy
4:12*

Evangelism

We get the words "evangelism" and "evangelical"
from the Greek word *euangélion*. A related Greek
word, *angelos*, means "messenger"; we get the English word "angel" from it, by way of *angelus*, its Latin
equivalent.
Euangélion is a message—specifically, a good
message. Translated into German, *euangélion* is *gut
spiel* (essentially, "good speak"), and translated into
Old English, *euangélion* is *gōd-spell*; this is where we
get the English word we use most often: *Gospel*.
Let's have a quick look at what Paul tells the

church at Rome about this good message (or in this translation, "Good News"):

> I have an obligation to those who are civilized and those who aren't, to those who are wise and those who aren't. I'm eager to tell you who live in Rome the Good News also. I'm not ashamed of the Good News. It is God's power to save everyone who believes, Jews first and Greeks as well. (Romans 1:14-16)

We can see two things in this little passage:

1. Paul is all about spreading the good message—the Gospel—of Jesus and is not afraid to be shameless about telling, well, everybody.

2. God's power to save is in the Gospel. *Power. To. Save.*

Here is the import of what I've just laid out in the last few paragraphs: evangelizing is *speaking God's power to save* into someone's life. Now, here are some truths about how to go about doing that:

To evangelize...

- you don't have to go to some far-off place—

although some have been called to do that, and you might also;

- you don't have to walk busy streets or lurk in cafeterias and parks and ask absolute strangers about spiritual matters—although some have been called to do that, and you might also;

- you don't have to know your Christian apologetics well enough to win an argument with an atheist— although knowing your Christian apologetics can't hurt. (But remember—only Jesus will change the atheist's heart, by the power of the Holy Spirit.)

To evangelize...

- you need to be ready when that budding disciple, that person to whom you have testified through your witness, that child, that lost and hurting person, or, perhaps, that total stranger demands to know what makes you the way you are. Peter says it simply and eloquently: "Always be ready to defend your confidence in God when anyone asks you to explain it" (1 Peter 3:15);

- when the time comes, just speak God's power to save into the life of that person who needs to know. You can do this without fear or shame. You can.

Ultimately, ideally, disciple-building and witness and evangelism are interrelated, and, in fact, inseparable from each other. When you disciple someone by teaching him or her what it's like to follow Jesus, you will most often also testify about Jesus' love through your daily witness—your response to the work of the Holy Spirit. And since the Holy Spirit will be at work on others as you disciple and as you witness, opportunities to share the *euangélion*—the good message about Jesus' death and resurrection and what these things mean—will follow as well.

Selected Bible passages related to evangelism: Romans 10:13-14; 1 Corinthians 15:1-4; 2 Corinthians 5:18-20; 2 Timothy 1:8; 2 Timothy 4:1-2

Summary

Let's step back and look at the big picture of disciple-building, witness and evangelism:

- Jesus invites us to disciple others wherever we go, whenever we go, whatever we do. Our job is to build relationships and demonstrate faithfully how Jesus is the center of our world view; the source and motivation for the way we live; the teacher we desire to follow and to emulate. We are to teach others what it means to follow Jesus.

- We need only to recognize opportunities to disciple in the courses of our lives, no matter where it is that we *go*. The course of your life may indeed take you to Indonesia or Ukraine or Sierra Leone or Peru or inner-city Detroit or Philadelphia; if it does, Jesus calls you to disciple there. Your life's course may not take you to an exotic place; but wherever you are, Jesus' call to disciple will be no different.

- Jesus is in charge of the belief part; you can entrust the soul of the person you're discipling to Him and to His Holy Spirit. However, Jesus does call you to be alert and open to the opportunity to share what you believe and why you believe it, as Peter writes: "Always be ready to defend your confidence in God when anyone asks you to explain it" (1 Peter 3:15).

Deal With It

1. Talk about some of Jesus' methods for disciple-building (for example, teaching through parables; teaching with authority; linking teaching to acts of compassion; or encouraging his disciples to do what He could do).

2. What's the difference between "Go! Make disciples of all nations…" and "Wherever you go, dis-

ciple all nations…"? Would you consider your-self a "Go!" type of person, or a "wherever you go" type of person? Talk about that; learn from each other.

3. What is the role of the Holy Spirit in discipling? In evangelism?

Go and Do

1. Think of someone who might be open to working with you to develop as a disciple (or to develop as disciples together!). Pray about discipling that person and watch for an opportunity to take a step in that direction. Remember that discipling is less about conversion than it is about showing someone what it's like to follow Jesus.

2. Teach yourself to tell your personal story of faith. Practice it with a friend or mentor.

Nine
What It All Could Look Like

The reality for all of us believers is that although God has called us, redeemed us and renewed us for life with Him, at this (early, earthly) stage of our eternal life, we are still broken people in a broken church that is reaching out to a broken world. This has three implications for believers:

1. During our time on earth, we will not become perfect disciples and the church will not become a perfect church. There will be failure, corruption, abuse, neglect, injustice, disappointment, pain, discouragement. You can be certain of it.

2. Knowing this can keep us honest—and humble. You and I are no better nor worse than the thief or the gambler or the addict or the liar who doesn't know Jesus yet—so we can all speak to each other as equals.

3. This is where Jesus does His work. He's in the business of fixing broken people and His broken church. He sends His Holy Spirit to the baptized Christian—and also to the thief and the gambler and the addict and the liar. He can transform you and me, no matter who we are. We can trust that He knows what He's doing.

With these truths in mind, we can begin to envision what the D360 life—whole-life, 360-degree discipleship—could look like in the individual believer, in the church, and in the eyes of the outsider.

Believer

The believer who embraces the D360 concept of whole-life discipleship will have a clear understanding that the good he or she does is a response to the work of the Holy Spirit and not works-righteousness —not deeds motivated by the misguided idea that those deeds will earn God's favor. People who know Jesus Christ as their Savior and Lord will also be confident that God sees His image restored in them through the finished work of Jesus.

Each believer will live his or her faith in tangible, dynamic ways in response to God's call to work alongside Him in His project to restore creation. There will be tremendous variety in the way this is played out. Some Christians will continue to respond to God's call to serve Him within the church as pastors, missionaries, deaconesses, teachers, and musicians; some will continue to respond by serving in the church as social ministry, communications, and technology professionals; clerical workers; health workers; ministry volunteers; and so on. Others will choose to live as whole-life disciples in non-church professions—science, technology, entertainment, education, legal or medical services, manufacturing, sales, engineering, waste management, public service, law enforcement, emergency management, and on and on—often influencing corporate and professional cultures by their service.

Whole-life disciples will respond to the Spirit's work through positive activism; rather than simply oppose evil, they will research and develop creative, compassionate ways to have an impact for good wherever good is needed. In his book *The Next Christians*, Gabe Lyons points to organizations such as To Write Love on Her Arms and the International Justice Mission as examples of this kind of activism. More examples might include Save the Storks (savethestorks.com), End Slavery Now (endslaverynow.org), and Advent Conspiracy (adventconspiracy.org).

Whole-life disciples will embrace whole-life worship—worship in their vocations; worship through the gifts they offer back to God in response to His goodness; and worship together with the faith community they belong to and with the members of their families. They will disciple and be discipled by other believers in the community. They will see—and seize—opportunities all around them to respond to God in worship. They will pour out their hearts to God in constant prayer and will experience astonishing growth in their knowledge of God and their trust in Him.

Whole-life disciples will preserve and protect human life. They will serve as faithful stewards of all of God's creation; of the everyday gifts He gives; and of the Gospel, His message of grace and hope for humanity.

Whole-life disciples will respond to God's call to disciple others. They will seek to build genuine relationships that can lead naturally to conversations about faith. They will be ready always to give a reason for the hope that they have. They will embrace opportunities to speak the *euangélion,* the Gospel. They will pray for the Spirit to exchange hearts of stone for hearts of flesh (cf. Ezekiel 36).

The church

The church will rededicate itself to serving as a training ground in discipleship. Churches will become less concerned about attracting and tracking members and more focused on building disciples.[1] Because fewer people who visit churches today have formal membership as their ultimate goal, the first option congregations provide to seekers or interested (or curious) visitors will no longer be the "New Member Class" that many have traditionally offered but rather an exploratory learning program that focuses on the essentials of faith, whole-life discipleship, and life in Christian community.

Congregations will also develop or adopt an array of disciple-building ministries of all kinds—service, activist, mentoring/coaching, body life (that is, life in the Body of Christ), worship arts, stewardship, prayer, teaching, leader development, and so on. Many churches will incorporate an intentional disciple-building time into their Sunday morning gathering cycles (This is where those new models I mentioned for developing discipling culture at the church level can be useful). Congregational small groups will focus on how God is calling individual disciples now—and how each individual is responding and learning and growing.

Congregations will celebrate and seek to develop believers' gifts, talents and abilities. They will help connect people's gifts where they can grow and do the most good. Congregations will lead the way in practicing sound financial stewardship by developing budgets and funding initiatives based on specific discipleship, evangelism and community needs.

Congregations will teach that weekly worship gatherings are part of a believer's whole-life worship —but they should never be seen as the only part. Congregations will uphold and celebrate giving—of time, effort, skill and financial gifts—as acts of worship.

Congregations will be welcoming, compassionate communities committed to joining God in His project of restoring creation. Congregations will call sin what it is; they will also preach redemption, and not only preach, but *practice*, renewal and restoration among broken people who are searching for hope and truth.

Congregations of the church will teach whole-life discipleship, whole-life worship and whole-life stewardship *as motivated by* the Gospel—not *instead of or in addition to* the Gospel.

Outsiders

Many people who have little or no exposure to Christian faith and Christian community don't know what you know about the church, don't have the frame of reference that you have. They may have seen and heard things that don't represent believers or what believers believe. As a result, they may have developed mistaken assumptions about these things.

A renewed focus on disciple-building can help change that. It will contribute to a sense among outsiders that the church and people who belong to it are engaged in all sorts of ministries that reflect the image of God by doing real good.

This renewed focus on disciple-building will help outsiders sense that the church is not so much about membership as it is about discipleship, not so much about conversion as about transformation. Churches will present outsiders with a path on which they can move naturally from curiosity/interest to involvement to training, mentoring and full participation in the life of the faith community. Outsiders will sense that belonging, inclusion and actualization are part of what involvement in Christian community is about.

Summary

Whole-life disciples will live what they believe, and the church will practice what it preaches. Much good will result. People outside the church will want to know what the deal is. Evangelism will result. The Spirit will do His work. God will be glorified.

Wrap-up

Be Who You're Called to Be

...you have put off the old self with its practices and have put on the new self, which is being renewed in knowledge after the image of its creator. Colossians 3:9b-10

So here's the wrap-up—you know, the part of the book that you read and say to yourself, "Well, why'd I read the first hundred fifty-plus pages when I could just have read this chapter and been done with it?" So ... if you've read the preceding hundred fifty-plus pages, you can skip this chapter if you want—*or* you can also use it to check that you understand 360-degree whole-life discipleship as I've explored it here.

The Core of D360 Whole-life Discipleship

My first aim was to frame the context within which these conversations would take place. I began with this concern: (1) Jesus' intent in His Great Commission was clearly that his disciples help others to develop into disciples; (2) many people—and churches—have reduced "building disciples" to "making members"—which is not necessarily the same thing; (3) many churches and organizations today have introduced exciting new efforts to reach out, but too many churches have done too little to get seekers involved in the process of disciple-building—and often fail ultimately to incorporate those seekers into their community. What all of us need—the church included—is a renewed focus on building disciples and involving them in the project of restoring God's kingdom.

Then I pointed to our motive for whole-life discipleship. Humans are the crowning achievement of God's act of creation, (1) uniquely fashioned in His image and imbued with many of the traits of His own character but (2) flawed and rebellious because humans chose to violate the boundaries He imposed. God refused to give up on his creation—including (especially!) us, his dearest creatures—and set in motion a project to restore it all, beginning with the image of Himself in us. He chose His own Son to become a human, Yahoshua (Jesus), and atone for humans' rebellion; and He gave His Holy Spirit the task of bringing human beings to faith in His bold plan. When faith is born in a person's heart, the Spirit enables and impels that person to respond

with his or her whole life and commit to living as a
disciple of Jesus.

What D360 Whole-life Discipleship Looks Like

My next aim was to envision discipleship as a 360
-degree commitment characterized by a number of
features:

Christian Learning. Discipleship is lifelong
learning—learning to know God; learning what redemption, restoration and renewal mean; learning to
be like Jesus. We learn from each other, but we learn
best from regular, careful study of God's Word in
the Bible. Look for big ideas in the Bible. Get a good
English translation (or learn Hebrew and Greek—
but really, a good translation presents a satisfactory
and much simpler path to deeper understanding).
Ask hard questions and then search for how God's
Word responds to them. Study with others. Don't be
surprised if, while finding an answer to a question,
you discover more questions. Trust God the Holy
Spirit to guide you.
  Living in Community. God exists in perfect eternal community; as creatures fashioned in His image,
we have the desire for relationship in our spiritual
and emotional DNA. God invites us into relationship
with Him. He wants to be part of our human rela-

tionships—marriage and family relationships, friendships, church relationships. We can learn—and our faith can grow—in each of these types of relationships. It is in relationships—particularly in the ways they can become damaged—that we come to a deeper understanding of how and why confession, forgiveness, and healing are important.

Dynamic Prayer. We have a special invitation from God to speak with Him—as a child does with his or her loving parent. We can pour out to Him everything we have on our hearts—our most rapturous joys, our gravest concerns, our deepest fears. When we have no words to express how we feel, He already knows. God wants our prayers to be sincere and heartfelt; He's not impressed by loads of fancy words. We use prayer to "seek God's face"—to meet Him up-close so He can show us His mind, His heart and His good will; so when we pray, we have the opportunity to know God better—and when we invite others to pray for us, *we offer them* the opportunity to know God better.

Whole-life Worship. That weekly time when we gather with other believers for an hour or two of praise, prayer, confession and God's gifts in His Word and sacraments is part of whole-life worship— but only part. We worship with our *lives* when we (1) point to God as the Master of all we are and our only Source of good; (2) respond to the Holy Spirit's work in us by desiring to learn and obey God's will; (3) invest the gifts and talents God has given us, great and not so great, in *service*—to God and to others; (4) offer back to God a portion of our finances and possessions; and (5) commit to holding one-on-one time with God. Like discipleship, worship is a whole-life thing.

Whole-life Stewardship. Although we have come to think of stewardship as something having to do with money and giving, stewardship is a much bigger thing. According to the creation account in Genesis, *humans were made to be stewards*—managers intended by God to work alongside Him in caring for and enjoying each other and the rest of His creation. God calls disciples of Jesus to serve as good stewards, making good use of the time, knowledge, gifts, talents, income and possessions He gives us, as well as protecting, preserving and caring for life and the world we live in. And He calls us to be good stewards of the *euangélion*, the Gospel, His amazing message of redemption and restoration through Jesus.

Helping Build More Disciples. When Jesus called his own disciples to be about the business of helping others become disciples, He was also calling every disciple who followed in their footsteps to do the same. We disciple when we show someone else what it's like to follow Jesus. Discipleship is often better "caught" than simply taught—and this happens best in relationships. Discipling is not necessarily the same thing as evangelizing—proclaiming the Gospel—but it typically (and naturally) leads to opportunities to evangelize.

That's it—really! God is at work on a project to restore all of His creation, beginning with the image of Himself in you and me. God has invited us to join Him in this project. How? By making us worthy of joining Him through the redemption that Jesus won for each of us by His death and resurrection ... AND through Jesus' command, "Wherever you go, make disciples of all nations: Baptize them in the name of the Father, and of the Son, and of the Holy Spirit. Teach them to do everything I have commanded you."

It's time. Be the disciple you're called to be. And as you go, help make more.

Big Ideas in The Bible

People have published extensive lists of the themes running through the Bible. My aim in this appendix is not to replicate other people's lists of themes or to produce the most comprehensive list of Bible themes ever. My list is what I think many people will agree are the Bible's major themes—its biggest ideas. You may think one or more of the big ideas I've listed doesn't belong here; or, more likely, you may think I've left off one or more big ideas that belong here. These are things we can bring up in the ongoing conversation at D360TheBlog.org.

God's Inspired Word. Paul tells Timothy that Scripture is "God-breathed"—that is, inspired by God (2 Timothy 3:16). Isaiah quotes Yahweh: "[My word] will accomplish whatever I want and achieve whatever I send it to do" (Isaiah 55:11). Our faith is rooted in the power of God's Word and in the reality and constancy of its Author.

Who God is. Who is created in whose image? One claim that skeptics make about the God of the Bible is that He's just too outrageous—there's no way rationally to understand why He behaves as He does.

Well, wouldn't you want *your* God to be something and do things that are beyond your ability to comprehend? A god who's not incomprehensible is not much of a god. No worries; our God is most certainly incomprehensible. Check out Isaiah 55 and Job 38-41.

Creation and God's purpose for humanity. God made everything for His own glory. When He made His greatest creation, humans, He made them to be His partners in managing what He had created. Read Genesis 1-2; read Job, including chapters 38-41, which you read in connection with the preceding big idea; read Psalm 8, Psalm 104 and Psalm 139.

Humanity's rebellion, its effects, and God's plan for redemption and restoration. Given the choice to obey or disobey the simple terms of God's first covenant, humans chose disobedience; this damaged their relationship with God, corrupted His image in them, and doomed them and their race to eternal separation from Him. But God didn't destroy or abandon them; instead, He set a plan in motion to restore humans. Phase 1 was completed when Jesus, God's promised Messiah, was born. Phase 2 was completed when Jesus died and then rose from the dead. Phase 3 is in progress. Check out Romans 3 and the book of Hebrews.

Faith. Faith is a key component in God's plan for redemption and restoration through Jesus as I described it in the preceding big idea. Faith is our trust in God's plan. God's Holy Spirit prepares our hearts, plants faith and starts it growing; we respond. Go back and read Romans 3 and the book of Hebrews again, plus Ephesians 2.

The Messiah, Messianic prophecies, and their fulfillment in Jesus. God promised that from the seed of Adam and Eve, there would be one born Whom He would anoint to set right what had gone wrong when humans chose disobedience and rebellion. God continued across the centuries to reinforce His promise about this Anointed One, this Messiah, through men He called to serve as His prophets. In the New Testament we learn that this promised Messiah is Jesus, who paid the price for the rebellion of all humanity with His death on a cross and then sealed the deal by returning from death to life. (Related big idea: *atonement*; look it up.)

Covenants and Obedience. During His last Passover supper with His disciples, Jesus identifies the cup He gives them after supper as the New Covenant in His blood (Luke 22:20). If this sounds momentous, it is. It would have seemed even more momentous—and portentous—to the disciples, who had grown up learning about the covenants that Yahweh had established with Noah, Abraham's family, Moses and David—because historically Israel's covenants with God served as the guidelines by which they understood their relationship with Him.

Law, Justice, Mercy, Grace, and the Gospel. God has given humanity His terms for living in harmony with Him; these have come to be known as His Law. God is perfectly just, so He administers and enforces those terms with perfect justice. Ultimately, His judgment would be eternally devastating for every human ever if He were not also perfectly merciful— willing to withhold judgment out of love and compassion for His dearest creation; in His mercy, God offers a second chance! Not only that, but He offers us this opportunity for restoration as a gift, for free; we call this God's *grace*. The *message* of God's grace is the *euangélion*, the Gospel. Check out Ephesians 2:1-6.

Be Witnesses ... Make Disciples. Jesus' two great commands prior to returning to be with the Father are "Disciple others wherever you go" and "You will be witnesses about me everywhere." Read Matthew 28 and Acts 1. And the rest of the New Testament.

The Church: the Body of Christ, the Bride of Christ. The term "church" is used in a variety of senses in the New Testament; when we use it in the phrase "the church," it most often refers to the whole number of true believers in Jesus as the Messiah. Jesus established the church (See Matthew 16:18, for example); God the Holy Spirit ignited the church movement during the festival of Shavuot (Pentecost) following Jesus' resurrection; the book of Acts narrates how the early church took root, grew and spread. The church is the focus of two of the most striking metaphors in Scripture, both constructed by Paul: *the Bride of Christ* and the *Body of Christ*. Check out Acts. Check out Romans 12, 1 Corinthians 12 and Ephesians 4 and 5.

Jesus' return ... the end ... and the new heaven and earth. In Matthew 24 and 25, Jesus prophesies his final coming (called the *parousia* by some churchy folks), when all people will be judged and the earth will come to an end. God will bring about a new heaven and a new earth. All true believers will be transformed (See 1 Corinthians 15) and united with Him for eternity. Although Jesus cautions that no one knows when in human time this will happen (Jesus claims that it will come as a thief in the night), the book of Revelation closes with Jesus' promise: "Yes! I'm coming soon!"

Notes

Introduction

1. Mike Breen, "Why the Missional Movement Will Fail," 12 September 2011, *Discipling Culture,* www.disciplingculture.com/why-the-missional-movement-will-fail.

One In the Image

1. Interestingly (perhaps), the word "Bible" simply means "book."

2. It's unfortunate and a little too convenient that we have Adam and Eve to blame for the choice to disobey God and corrupt the nature of all humankind ever afterward (particularly Adam—see Romans 5:12). If the serpent had failed in his first attempt to trick Adam and Eve into choosing disobedience, he would not have given up; and if Adam and Eve managed to continue resisting, he would have targeted the children that Adam and Eve would bring into the world. Every human is born with the same freedom to choose; someone was bound to choose poorly. It's apparent from Scripture that

God was aware of the inevitability of this; when He told the humans His conditions for living in the Garden, He said, "You are free to eat from any tree in the garden. But you must never eat from the tree of the knowledge of good and evil because when you eat from it, you will certainly die" (Genesis 2:16-17). Note that He said *when*, not *if*. He was not surprised by Adam and Eve's choice; nor is He surprised when you and I choose to disobey Him.

3. Not everybody agrees that the image of God in humans includes the human conscience. In the Romans passage, Paul assumes that non-Jews can obey God's laws *by nature*. The process of deduction leads us to ask, what is it in the *nature* of both Jews and non-Jews that connects them to the same source of moral law? The image of God fills that bill. Unless conscience is a separate, unrelated, unique thing, it's reasonable to suppose that conscience belongs to the image of God in humans. Is the human conscience perfect? Of course not. Is the image of God in humans perfect? According to what I've laid out here, no, not since the first humans rejected God's terms for living in the garden. This is not proof that the image of God in a human being includes his or her conscience; it merely demonstrates that the argument for such a conclusion holds up.

Two Discipleship: A Life of Response to the Work of the Holy Spirit

1. Martin Luther, The Small Catechism. St. Louis: Concordia Publishing House, 1986. http://catechism.cph.org/en/creed.html.

2. Kyle Idleman, *not a fan*, Grand Rapids, Mich.: Zondervan, 2011.

3. "Best practice," www.dictionary.com.

4. www.youtube.com/user/NOOMAtube

Three Christian Learning: Understanding God's Word

1. There is some disagreement as to how the name is actually pronounced. When it is written, it consists of four Hebrew letters, yod-he-waw-he/yud-heh-vav-heh (HWHY). Often it is referred to as the Tetragrammaton (four letters). A significant number of scholars assent that "Yahweh" is the most likely pronunciation.

2. Names of God Bible, Grand Rapids, Mich.: Baker Publishing Group, 2011. Or go to www.biblegateway.com/versions/Names-of-God-NOG-Bible.

Four Community: God, You and Others

1. The phrase "One What, three Who's" is generally attributed to theologian Millard Erickson.

2. David H. Stern, tr. Complete Jewish Bible. Clarksville, Md.: Lederer Messianic Publications, 1998.

Five Prayer: Your Direct Access to the God Who Listens

1. New King James Version, Nashville, TN: Thomas Nelson, 1982.

2. For a review of Luther's teaching on The Lord's Prayer, go here: bookofconcord.org/smallcatechism.php#lordsprayer.

3. Joel D. Fredrich, "The Lord's Prayer: Exegesis of Matthew 6:9-13 and Luke 11:2-4," 2010. http://www.wlsessays.net/bitstream/handle/123456789/1648/FredrichLordsPrayer.pdf

4. The Holy Bible, New International Version, Biblica, Inc., 1973, 1978, 1984, 2011.

5. Others might argue that in allowing the fatally ill

loved one to die, God has in fact granted the believer's prayer by curing the loved one perfectly, forever. And of course those who die in faith do receive God's perfect healing! However, I suspect most of those who have prayed for the healing of their sick loved one would object that their particular prayers had not been granted because the perfect, eternal healing of their loved one was not the specific outcome they were asking for.

Six Worship: It Might Not Be What You Think. It's More.

1. Matt Boswell, ed., "What is Worship?" TGC Worship, The Gospel Coalition, http://blogs.thegospelcoalition.org/tgcworship/2013/10/11/what-is-worship.

2. For more on this teaching, visit the Vocation section of The Lutheran Church—Missouri Synod's online Life Library, www.lcms.org/page.aspx?pid=870.

3. Just a quick note about the term *confess*: it's used in two different ways by Christians and throughout the Bible. *Confess* is derived from a Latin word that means "say with" or "say the same thing." In its first sense, *confess* is used to describe when

someone says the same thing about God that God says about Himself. That is, when we confess our faith, we agree with Scripture's characterization of the triune God, with the claim that Jesus was fully God and fully human and that he died for our sins and rose again, and so on. In its second sense, *confess* is used to mean "agree" or "acknowledge"; when we confess our sins, we acknowledge that something we have done in violation of God's will is indeed a sin. The Greek word commonly translated as *confess* is *homologeo*, which means, literally, to conclude the same thing together. Several Hebrew words are translated as *confess* in the Old Testament: *yada, yadah,* and *nadad.*

Seven Stewardship: It's NOT (all) About Money?

1. Gabe Lyons, *The Next Christians: Seven Ways You Can Live the Gospel and Restore the World*. Colorado Springs: Multnomah Books, 2010, 53.

2. Alvin L. Barry, "What About Christian Stewardship?" www.lcms.org/document.fdoc?src=lcm&id=1096, n.d.

3. I thought it would be good here to add a note about the churchy word "Law." This will not be a long theological treatise, but it's worthwhile to ex-

plain that when Dr. Barry uses the term "Law," he
is referring to a central understanding in Christian
theology. According to the handy *Cyclopedia* provided by The Lutheran Church—Missouri Synod,
the Law is "a divine doctrine which reveals the
righteousness and immutable will of God, shows
how man ought to be disposed in his nature,
thoughts, words, and deeds in order to be pleasing
and acceptable to God, and threatens the transgres-
sors of the law with God's wrath and temporal and
eternal punishment" (cyclopedia.lcms.org/
display.asp?t1=L&word=LAWANDGOSPEL).
The Gospel, as I have described it, stands in contrast to the Law, absolving believers of their guilt
on account of Jesus' finished work of atonement.

**Eight Disciple-building. And Witness. And Evan-
gelism.**

1. Alan Hirsch, *Disciplism: Reimagining Evangelism
   Through the Lens of Discipleship*. Exponential Resources, 2014.

2. Here it's worthwhile to point out a common mis-
   conception about faith groups that practice infant
   baptism. In the minds of some believers, the baptism of an infant has been misconstrued to be a su-
   perstitious ritual that devotees believe will confer

salvation without the need for faith—and without the need for disciple-building as well. But many of those who consider baptism a sacrament *agree* that faith in God's grace given through the death and resurrection of Jesus is necessary for salvation. What they also believe is that the Holy Spirit has power to work living, active faith in the heart and soul of an infant who cannot speak or even think. That's the *sacrament* part: it's God the Holy Spirit's power, not the ritual, that creates faith and secures forgiveness and salvation—which means that what happens in the baptism of an infant is a true act of God. We can't comprehend it—but we can respond to God's invitation to participate in it.

In any event, discipling is always expected to follow the baptism of the infant. No matter what miracle has happened in a person's heart and soul through the sacrament of baptism, the person's faith will languish if there is no attempt to support his or her faith with careful discipling.

Peter answered them, "All of you must turn to God and change the way you think and act, and each of you must be baptized in the name of Jesus Christ so that your sins will be forgiven. Then you will receive the Holy Spirit as a gift. This promise belongs to you and to your children and to everyone who is far away." (Acts 2:38-39)

Nine What It All Could Look Like

1. No doubt this will be challenging for many
    churches that have employed a membership sys-
    tem time out of mind—but especially challeng-
    ing, at least at the outset, for churches whose con-
    fessions tie core elements of church life, such as
    the sacrament of communion, to membership. I
    believe that as they shift to an intensive focus on
    disciple-building, most churches will be able to
    deal effectively with whatever challenges present
    themselves. A little plain-spoken instruction dur-
    ing worship gatherings that incorporate the sac-
    rament of communion will also go a long way.

Acknowledgments

I am indebted to a number of people who contributed valuable time and effort to the development and publication of this resource. I am especially grateful for the input of Rev. Brad Urlaub and my other colleagues on the Lutheran Campus Mission Association's Board of Directors, as well as for the helpful feedback provided by Rebecca Hawthorne and Eric Shafer.

A great big thanks also to those who offered encouraging words during the writing process and those who shared their enthusiasm about D360 with others even before the resource was published. Every author should have such friends!

And whatever glory comes of this D360 project, let it all go to our loving God, Who has invited us into His project to restore His creation and the image of Himself in each of us.

About the Author

Greg Koenig is a preacher's kid, educator and writer who has dedicated a lot of his adult life to understanding and interpreting faith and the Christian experience from the perspective of someone unacquainted with churchspeak (often also called *Christianese*). "The phrase *image of God* in this book is a good example," says Greg. "Many of us insiders love to use the term *imago Dei*, which is the Latin equivalent of the Hebrew *b'tzelem Elohim*—image, or shadow, or likeness of God. There is an elegance and a mystique to the phrase *imago Dei*, but the elegance and mystique are not particularly helpful to someone who is just learning to respond to the message of the Bible. That simple message from God needs to strike a chord and then resonate; the language we use must allow it to do that."

Greg is the servant-leader of the Lutheran Campus Mission Association (GoLCMA.org), an organization dedicated to equipping leaders to reach out with the Gospel in college/university communities. He lives in St. Louis, Missouri and has four children and five grandchildren.

60928601R00104

Made in the USA
Charleston, SC
12 September 2016